Honolulu
& Oahu
DIRECTIONS

WRITTEN AND RESEARCHED BY

Greg Ward and Samantha Cook

ROUGH
GUIDES

NEW YORK • LONDON • DELHI
www.roughguides.com

Contents

Introduction to

Honolulu
& Oahu

◄ Surfboard at Duke's Canoe Club

Although Oahu is only the third largest of the Hawaiian islands – its six hundred square miles are dwarfed by the four thousand square miles of the aptly named Big Island – it's home to just over 900,000 people, or roughly three-quarters of the state's population. Half of those live along a narrow strip of Oahu's southeast coast, in the city of Honolulu, while the powerhouse that keeps the Hawaiian economy going is even smaller and more crowded – tiny Waikīkī, three miles east of downtown.

After a century of mass tourism, the very name of Waikīkī continues to epitomize beauty, sophistication, and glamor. Of course, squeezing enough tower blocks to hold one hundred thousand hotel beds into

▼ Lū'au pork dish

▲ Surfers at Waikīkī Beach

a mere two square miles leaves little room for unspoiled tropical scenery. The legendary beach, however, remains irresistible, and Waikīkī offers a full-on resort experience to match any in the world. Around five million visitors per year spend their days on the sands of Waikīkī, and their nights in its hotels, restaurants, and bars; for many of them, barring the odd expedition to the nearby Ala Moana shopping mall, the rest of Honolulu might just as well not exist.

All of which suits the average citizen of Honolulu just fine. Honolulu is a distinctive and remarkably attractive city in its own right. The setting is gorgeous, stretching back from the ocean into a succession of spectacularly lush valleys cut into the dramatic *pali* (cliffs) of the Ko'olau Mountains. Downtown Honolulu, centered around a group of administrative buildings that date from the final days of the Hawaiian monarchy, nestles at the foot of the extinct Punchbowl

When to go

Of all the major US cities, Honolulu is said to have both the lowest average maximum temperature and the highest minimum, at 85°F and 60°F respectively. Neither fluctuates more than a few degrees between summer and winter. Waikīkī remains a balmy tropical year-round resort, and the only seasonal variation likely to make much difference to travelers is the state of the surf on the North

▲ BIRD OF PARADISE

Shore. For surfers, the time to come is from October to April, when mighty winter waves scour the sand off many beaches and come curling in at heights of twenty feet or more. In summer, the surf-bums head off home, and some North Shore beaches are even safe for family swimming.

As for room rates, peak season in Waikīkī runs from December to March, and many mid-range hotels lower their prices by anything from ten to thirty dollars at other times. Waikīkī is pretty crowded all year, though, and there are few savings to be made by coming in summer.

▲ Vintage menu cover, Hawaii Maritime Center

volcano, now a military cemetery. As well as boasting top-quality museums such as the Bishop Museum and the Academy of Arts, the city also offers superb rainforest hikes, especially in Makiki and Mānoa valleys.

What's more, thanks to massive immigration, Honolulu's population is among the most ethnically diverse in the world. Fewer than ten percent of its inhabitants consider themselves "Native Hawaiians;" some 42 percent claim Asian ancestry, 26 percent identify themselves as Caucasian, and twenty percent see themselves as mixed.

Just across the Ko'olaus from Honolulu, the green cliffs of the windward coast are magnificent, lined with safe, secluded beaches and indented with remote time-for-gotten valleys. Further north, Oahu's North Shore is the world's premier surfing destination; Waimea, Sunset and 'Ehukai beaches are compelling spectacles, while the funky little town of Hale'iwa makes a refreshing contrast to Waikīkī.

◄ Sunset cocktails at the Beach Bar

Honolulu & Oahu
AT A GLANCE

WAIKĪKĪ

In a sense, Waikīkī is just a squashed-up suburb of Honolulu; for tourists, though, it's very much the tail that wags the dog, housing, feeding, and entertaining a hundred thousand visitors per night, and boasting enough beach space to accommodate the lot by day.

▲ Waikīkī Beach

▲ Surfing at Sunset Beach

THE NORTH SHORE

Considering its reputation among the world's surfers, Oahu's legendary North Shore is amazingly under-developed. Apart from one small town, funky little Hale'iwa, it's just a long strip of glorious sandy beach, pounded in winter by ferocious waves that only true experts can ride.

DOWNTOWN HONOLULU

Stretched out at the foot of the mountains, circled by volcanic craters, downtown Honolulu is a surprisingly quiet and stately district, filled with monuments to Hawaii's much-lamented former monarchy.

▲ Hawaii State Art Museum, Downtown Honolulu

▲ Lei shop, Chinatown

HANAUMA BAY

Less than ten miles from downtown Honolulu, Hanauma Bay is Hawaii's premier snorkeling destination, but even if you never put your head under the water it's a fabulous spot, with its long curving beach sheltered inside what's left of an extinct volcano.

▼ Hanauma Bay

CHINATOWN

Traditionally the liveliest of Honolulu's neighborhoods, bursting with food markets, quirky little stores, and amazing flower shops, Chinatown is currently also the hippest, with up-to-the minute restaurants, bars, and galleries opening all the time.

WINDWARD OAHU

Cross the mountains east from Honolulu, and you're in another world, of magnificent sheer cliffs, stunning empty beaches, and time-forgotten rainforest valleys.

▼ Kailua Beach, Windward Oahu

Ideas

The big six

If you imagine that one tropical resort is pretty much like another, the sheer variety of landscapes and experiences that Oahu has to offer will take your breath away. Whether you're a surfer, swimmer, sunbather, or snorkeler, the Pacific Ocean has to be the main attraction, but there's also a wealth of history, heritage, and, of course, heavenly Hawaiian music to savor. To get the full flavor of Hawaii, just be sure to get out of Honolulu at least once during your stay.

▲ Bishop Museum

By far the best place to learn about Hawaii and its Polynesian past.

P.113 ▸ THE PALI AND LIKELIKE HIGHWAYS

▲ Hanauma Bay

Cradled in an extinct volcanic crater, this lovely crescent bay offers Oahu's best snorkeling.

P.122 ▸ SOUTHEAST OAHU

▶ **Waikīkī Beach**

The world's most famous beach makes an irresistible first stop for every fresh-off-the-plane new arrival.

P.45 ▸ WAIKĪKĪ

▲ **Surfing the North Shore**

The home of surfing remains its greatest arena, drawing winter crowds of spectators as well as participants.

P.146 ▸ THE NORTH SHORE

▼ **USS Arizona Memorial**

An evocative monument to a seminal moment in US history, spanning the devastated battleship in the waters of Pearl Harbor.

P.115 ▸ PEARL HARBOR

▲ **Hawaiian music**

No trip to Hawaii is complete without enjoying the talents of the islands' legendary musicians.

P.22 ▸ IDEAS

Beaches

Waikīkī is merely the most famous of dozens of magnificent beaches that ring the island of Oahu. Its see-and-be-seen buzz and round-the-clock activity make it a fabulous resort destination, but elsewhere on the island you'll find plenty of prettier beaches, on some of which you may even turn out to be the only human being in sight. The beaches listed here are the most attractive, and most suited for simple family fun; the great surfing beaches are listed overleaf.

▲ Waimānolo Beach

Tucked away in Oahu's southeast corner, this long, idyllic beach usually holds just a few scattered locals, with barely a tourist in sight.

P.125 ▸ SOUTHEAST OAHU

▼ Waikīkī Beach

Whether it's to ride an outrigger canoe, or stroll in the moonlight, you'll find you can't stay away from the beach in Waikīkī.

P.45 ▸ WAIKĪKĪ

▲ Kuilima Cove

Nestling alongside the Turtle Bay Resort, Kuilima Cove offers perfect family sunning and swimming.

P.147 ▸ THE NORTH SHORE

▼ Kailua Beach Park

The jewel of the Windward shore, a glorious gently shelving strand lapped by turquoise waters.

P.131 ▸ WINDWARD OAHU

▶ Magic Island

Just minutes from Waikīkī, this sheltered artificial crescent of sand is one of Honolulu's best-kept secrets.

P.91 ▸ WATERFRONT HONOLULU

Hawaii's Polynesian heritage

Hawaii has been Polynesian for far longer than it's been American. The traces of its ancient past are not always immediately apparent, but they're definitely still there if you know where to look. While the Bishop Museum is an unparalleled resource for visitors who want to know more about pre-contact Hawaii, only by seeking out Oahu's ancient shrines and temples can you experience the lingering *mana* or spiritual power of the Polynesian ancestors.

▼ Bishop Museum

The world's finest collection of ancient Hawaiian artifacts, plus fascinating displays from all over Polynesia.

P.113 ▸ THE PALI AND LIKELIKE HIGHWAYS

▼ Kāne'āki Heiau

Hawaii's most thoroughly restored ancient temple, hidden away in Mākaha Valley on the Leeward Shore.

P.160 ▸ LEEWARD OAHU

◀ Polynesian Cultural Center

Crafts, performances, games, and architecture from seven Pacific island groups – great fun, so long as you take it all with a pinch of salt.

P.137 ▶ WINDWARD OAHU

▲ The Hōkūle'a

The exploits of this replica canoe, based at the Hawaii Maritime Center, have sparked renewed interest in ancient Polynesian voyaging.

P.90 ▶ WATERFRONT HONOLULU

▼ Pu'u O Mahuka State Monument

Poised high above the North Shore, this ancient war temple was once home to fearsome tattooed warriors.

P.145 ▶ THE NORTH SHORE

Museums and historic sites

In just over two centuries, Hawaii has made the transition from a chain of warring chiefdoms via a stable monarchy to incorporation into the United States. Relics of those years give Honolulu a fascinating assortment of historical monuments, from the only royal palace in the United States to the site of the Japanese attack on Pearl Harbor – and as a cultural crossroads it also holds some wonderful art from all over the world.

▲ Honolulu Academy of Arts

A delightful architectural gem that houses a stunning collection of art from all over the world.

P.76 ▸ DOWNTOWN HONOLULU

▲ USS Arizona Memorial

Take a boat trip across Pearl Harbor to remember the "date which will live in infamy."

P.115 ▸ PEARL HARBOR

◀ Hawaii's Plantation Village

This restored community in central Oahu tells the story of how agricultural laborers from around the globe shaped the face of today's Hawaii.

P.153 ▸ CENTRAL OAHU

▼ Contemporary Museum

Set in beautiful gardens in the rainforest overlooking Honolulu, the Contemporary Museum plays host to stimulating temporary exhibitions.

P.101 ▸ MAKIKI AND MĀNOA

◀ 'Iolani Palace

At the heart of downtown Honolulu, this imposing former palace evokes all the romance and tragedy of Hawaii's last monarchs.

P.70 ▸ DOWNTOWN HONOLULU

▶ The Mission Houses

Simple stone houses in downtown Honolulu marking the spot where missionaries from New England set about changing Hawaii forever.

P.75 ▸ DOWNTOWN HONOLULU

Accommodation

The fact that almost all visitors to Oahu stay in Waikīkī ensures that it holds something to suit everyone, from world-class luxury hotels like the *Halekūlani* to charming historic veterans like the *Royal Hawaiian*, and from large, efficient, family-oriented chain hotels to lively budget hostels. It is, however, possible to stay elsewhere on the island. Spending a few nights on the North Shore offers a very different perspective, whether you do it on the cheap or in the lazy opulence of the remote *Turtle Bay Resort*.

▲ Halekūlani

If money's no object, stay at this magnificent oceanfront hotel, which has to be the most luxurious option in Waikīkī.

P.170 ▶ ACCOMMODATION

▲ Outrigger and Ohana hotels

Offering a dozen well-priced hotels between them, these closely connected chains are the most dependable family and mid-range options in Waikīkī.

P.169 ▶ ACCOMMODATION

▼ Hawaiiana Hotel

A genuine throwback to a more innocent
era, Waikīkī's most appealing budget hotel is
filled with *tiki* statues and 1950s charm.

P.165 ▸ ACCOMMODATION

▲ The Royal Hawaiian

All glamor and retro elegance, the 1920s
"Pink Palace" remains the atmospheric focal
point of Waikīkī Beach.

P.171 ▸ ACCOMMODATION

▶ Backpacker's Vacation Inn

A North Shore institution, with accommodation ranging from dorm beds for surf bums
up to private beachfront apartments.

P.174 ▸ ACCOMMODATION

▼ Turtle Bay Resort

Superbly relaxing full-service resort on the
North Shore, in a breathtaking location with
very different secluded bays to either side.

P.174 ▸ ACCOMMODATION

Scenic spots

Few cities in the world can boast a more beautiful setting than Honolulu, stretching languidly between the mountains and the ocean, fringed with golden beaches, watered by countless streams, and scattered with ancient volcanic cones. The rest of the island is even more spectacular, especially along the eroded Windward shore, where millennia of erosion have sculpted awesome sheer cliffs and lush, sinuous valleys.

▼ Pu'u 'Ualaka'a Park

High in the rainforest above Honolulu, this tiny park offers the best views over the city.

P.104 ▶ MAKIKI AND MĀNOA

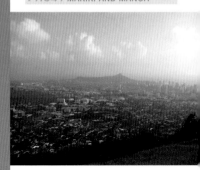

▼ Mokoli'i Island

Oahu's Windward shore is dotted with little islets, none more picturesque than conical Mokoli'i.

P.134 ▶ WINDWARD OAHU

▲ Byōdō-In Temple

Gloriously peaceful Japanese temple, set in tranquil gardens at the foot of the Ko'olau Mountains.

P.133 › WINDWARD OAHU

◄ Nu'uanu Pali State Park

The one place where you can see the whole majesty of Oahu's Windward cliffs stretching off towards the horizon.

P.112 › THE PALI AND LIKELIKE HIGHWAYS

▼ Diamond Head

The extinct volcanic cone of Diamond Head, dominating the Waikīkī skyline, is Hawaii's most famous landmark.

P.66 › KAPI'OLANI PARK AND DIAMOND HEAD

Hawaiian music

Could anyone come to Hawaii and not fall in love with Hawaiian music? As home to many of the islands' finest musicians, Oahu is the perfect place to see them performing live. You won't regret seeking them out, though whether it's the veteran greats of the past, still going strong, or the rising stars of today, you may have to venture out of Waikīkī to do so.

▼ Auntie Genoa Keawe

Every Thursday night, octogenarian falsetto singer Auntie Genoa offers Waikīkī's biggest weekly musical treat.

P.61 ▶ WAIKĪKĪ

▼ Blue Hawaii

If it was Elvis who made you want to come to Hawaii in the first place, you'll love Jonathan von Brana's tongue-in-cheek Waikīkī revue.

P.61 ▶ WAIKĪKĪ

▶ Eddie Kamae

Founder with the great Gabby Pahinui of the Sons of Hawaii, ukulele legend Eddie Kamae hosts delightful weekly jam sessions for a lively local crowd in a little-known Windward haunt.

P.140 ▶ WINDWARD OAHU

▲ House Without a Key

With their ravishing sunset setting, the nightly hula shows at Waikīkī's loveliest beachfront bar are a fabulous no-cover treat.

P.60 ▶ WAIKĪKĪ

▼ Chai's

Thai restaurant by Honolulu Harbor that showcases the finest contemporary Hawaiian musicians every night of the year.

P.98 ▶ WATERFRONT HONOLULU

Hikes

Honolulu isn't all beaches, and it isn't all traffic and high-rise hotels. If you're looking for wilderness, you will find great rainforest trails to enjoy within a mile or two of downtown, and even towering waterfalls. Be sure to take your hiking gear with you as you explore the rest of the island, too, as the Windward shore in particular holds a succession of fabulous "lost" valleys.

▲ Diamond Head

Locals do it more for exercise than for fun, but for visitors the novelty of climbing through mysterious tunnels in a long-dead volcano makes the haul up Diamond Head worthwhile.

P.66 ▸ KAPI'OLANI AND DIAMOND HEAD

▲ Kahana Valley

Still farmed in traditional Hawaiian style, Kahana Valley also offers some great ocean-view hiking.

P.134 ▸ WINDWARD OAHU

▲ Makiki Valley

A network of spectacular trails lace through the dense rainforest in the hills above Honolulu.

P.102 ▶ MAKIKI AND MĀNOA

▼ Mānoa Falls

Oahu's most popular short hike leads to a dramatic waterfall at the far end of Mānoa Valley, just a few miles from Waikīkī.

P.105 ▶ MAIKIKI AND MĀNOA

◀ Maunawili Falls Trail

Criss cross a broad stream deep in the windward hills, push your way through resplendent flowering vegetation, and you'll be rewarded by reaching the low but attractive Maunawili Falls.

P.130 ▶ WINDWARD OAHU

▼ Hau'ula

The best place to penetrate deep into the sheer-walled, time-forgotten valleys of Windward Oahu.

P.136 ▶ WINDWARD OAHU

Oahu for kids

It's hard to imagine any child could get bored with the beaches and ocean sports of Oahu. Just supposing, though, the kids grow tired of being cooped up in some Waikīkī tower block, and fancy looking for adventure elsewhere on the island, then the choice of activities and attractions is endless.

▼ USS Missouri

Kids love to explore the "Mighty Mo," the world's last battleship, from the massive guns on deck to the engine rooms down below.

P.119 ▶ PEARL HARBOR

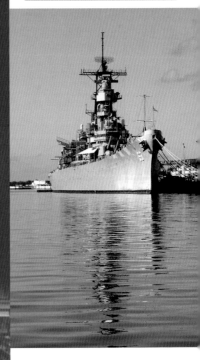

▼ Kualoa Ranch

A host of land and ocean adventures for kids, from horse-riding to kayaking.

P.134 ▶ WINDWARD OAHU

▲ Hawaiian Waters Adventure Park

Hawaii's only water park is around an hour's drive out of Waikīkī, but it's packed with slides and pools.

P.157 ▸ LEEWARD OAHU

▼ Science Adventure Center

What child could resist the gigantic volcano, spouting hot "lava" on demand, that dominates the Bishop Museum's latest addition.

P.114 ▸ THE PALI AND LIKELIKE HIGHWAYS

▶ Dole Plantation

With a baffling maze for older kids, and a train ride for the younger ones, the Dole Plantation makes a welcome break in the circle-island drive.

P.154 ▸ CENTRAL OAHU

Gourmet restaurants

Honolulu's restaurant scene is buzzing. By drawing on the best of both Asian and American contemporary cuisine, Hawaii's top chefs have created their own compelling fusion, often known as "Hawaii Regional" but closely approximating what travelers may already know as "Pacific Rim." The emphasis is on fresh island ingredients, and especially fish, delicately prepared and flavored with Asian herbs and spices.

▲ Ola

This lovely little restaurant, alongside the *Turtle Bay Resort*, pretty much has the gorgeous beach at Kuilima Cove to itself each evening, and serves modern Hawaiian cuisine in a romantic, laidback atmosphere.

P.150 ▸ WINDWARD OAHU

▲ Indigo Eurasian Cuisine

Chinatown's smartest, buzziest restaurant, where everything is given a contemporary twist and the attention to detail is a joy.

P.84 ▸ CHINATOWN

▼ Sansei

Truly memorable, and very well-priced sushi and Pacific Rim specialties just a few steps from Waikīkī Beach.

P.58 ▶ WAIKĪKĪ

▲ Orchids

Both the gourmet Asian–Hawaiian cuisine and the oceanfront setting are absolutely perfect in this seafood-lover's dream, in Waikīkī's smartest hotel.

P.58 ▶ WAIKĪKĪ

◄ Alan Wong's

Superb modern Hawaiian cuisine, hidden away not far from the University; for a real extravaganza, order Mr Wong's nightly tasting menu.

P.106 ▶ MAKIKI AND MĀNOA

▶ Sam Choy's Diamond Head

Gleaming, fancy "New Hawaiian" restaurant, run by local favorite Sam Choy, a mile from the bustle of Waikīkī; be sure to sample Sam's fried poke.

P.69 ▶ KAPIʻOLANI PARK AND DIAMOND HEAD

Affordable eating

Home to immigrants from all over the world, and thronging daily with hungry tourists, Honolulu offers something to satisfy every palate. The options are almost limitless, with every imaginable kind of Asian fast food in Chinatown, cheap Japanese noodle bars in Waikīkī, and "local" diners of all kinds scattered throughout the city, not to mention the Italian, Chinese, and Mexican restaurants you'd expect in any international resort.

PORK
돼지고기
豚肉

▲ Ruffage Natural Foods

A winning two-in-one Waikīkī combination of healthy wholefoods deli by day, and tasty sushi bar by night.

P.58 ▸ WAIKĪKĪ

▲ OnJin's Café

This friendly little café, specializing in serious food at silly prices, makes a welcome break if you're shopping nearby at Honolulu's main shopping malls.

P.97 ▸ WATERFRONT HONOLULU

▲ Kaka'ako Kitchen

A local favorite for its quickfire but always tasty Hawaiian-style lunches and dinners, ranging from Asian specialties to all-American diner food.

P.96 ▸ WATERFRONT HONOLULU

▶ Yakiniku Camellia Buffet

Inexpensive Korean barbecue place near the University, where you choose fresh ingredients from the refrigerated cabinets then grill them yourself at your table.

P.107 ▸ MAKIKI AND MĀNOA

◀ Todai Seafood Buffet

High-quality, all-you-can-eat Japanese food in Waikīkī – including hand-made sushi, sashimi, noodles, and *teppanyaki* – at very reasonable prices.

P.59 ▸ WAIKĪKĪ

Bars and clubs

When the cocktail hour approaches, when the sun drops toward the horizon, or when the air just seems too balmy for you to go back to your hotel room just yet, Waikīkī and Honolulu hold a fine assortment of bars where the hours can simply melt away.

▲ Duke's Canoe Club

Packed with vintage surfing memorabilia and redolent with the flavor of years gone by, this is a beach bar with atmosphere.

P.60 ▸ WAIKĪKĪ

▲ Hank's Café

Chinatown's liveliest and most cosmopolitan bar, with an arty crowd downstairs and hip jazz fans on the second floor.

P.86 ▸ CHINATOWN

◀ Hula's

Despite changes of venue, Waikiki's longest standing gay club is a true Oahu institution, which goes out of its way to welcome its weekly influx of neophyte visitors.

P.59 ▸ WAIKĪKĪ

▼ La Mariana Sailing Club

Possibly Hawaii's last authentic *tiki* bar, hidden away in Honolulu Harbor, *La Mariana* abounds in 1950s Hawaiiana, and is renowned for its weekly old-time singalongs.

P.98 ▸ WATERFRONT HONOLULU

◀ Beach Bar

A romantic venue for a leisurely sunset cocktail, facing Waikīkī Beach from the landscaped lawns of the century-old *Moana Surfrider Hotel*.

P.60 ▸ WAIKĪKĪ

Surfing spots

Nowhere in the world has the same cachet for surfers as Oahu's North Shore; tackling the big waves of Hawaii is the dream of every aficionado of the sport. What often surprises casual visitors is how beautiful the great surfing beaches are, and what a joy it can be to sit on the sand as the sun goes down and watch the professionals hone their skills just a few yards offshore.

▲ Waimea Bay Beach County Park

With its consistently enormous waves, in winter at any rate, Waimea Bay is strictly for experts only.

P.144 ▶ THE NORTH SHORE

▲ Sunset Beach

The prettiest of the major surfing beaches, as you might expect Sunset Beach fills up daily, with serious surfers and awestruck spectators, in time for its spectacular namesake sunsets.

P.146 ▶ THE NORTH SHORE

▲ Mākaha Beach

Though home to several major surf competitions, Leeward Oahu's premier surf spot remains for most of the year the preserve of daredevil locals.

P.159 ▶ LEEWARD OAHU

▶ Waikīkī Beach

Modern landscaping work has ensured that the surf at Waikīkī is not what it was, but for pilgrims and beginners alike surfing here remains a right of passage.

P.45 ▶ WAIKĪKĪ

▼ 'Ehukai Beach Park

Home to the tubular waves of the legendary Banzai Pipeline, just offshore, 'Ehukai is the ideal vantage point to admire surfing stunts from the safety of the sand.

P.146 ▶ THE NORTH SHORE

Hawaiian food and drink

Although Hawaii belongs to the United States, there's still plenty that's distinctively Hawaiian. The best place to sample traditional foods like *kālua* pork is at a commercial *lū'au*, while the favorite dishes introduced to the islands by generations of immigrants feature on the menus of "local" diners all over the island.

▲ Cocktails

What more could you want from a trip to Hawaii than to drink a Mai Tai out of a pineapple at sunset?

P.183 ▸ ESSENTIALS

▼ Poi

The authentic taste of old Hawaii; you have to try this purple taro-root paste at least once, even if you agree with Captain Cook that it's a "disagreeable mess."

P.182 ▸ ESSENTIALS

▶ Kālua pork at a lūʻau

Baked all day in an underground oven, shredded *kālua* pork, reminiscent of Southern barbecued hog, is a highlight of any *lūʻau*.

P.182 ▸ ESSENTIALS

◀ Shave ice

These rainbow-colored concoctions of syrup-smothered ice are big business on Oahu, and nowhere more so than at Haleʻiwa.

P.144 ▸ THE NORTH SHORE

▼ Shrimp stands

The North and windward shores of Oahu are lined with colorful roadside vans and stalls, selling succulent fresh shrimp.

P.139 ▸ WINDWARD OAHU

▶ Saimin

If Hawaii has a national dish these days, it's *saimin*, or noodle soup; you can buy a bowl for under $5 in cafés all over the island.

P.182 ▸ ESSENTIALS

Ocean fun

Swimming and surfing are the obvious things to do when you're first let loose in the Pacific Ocean, but there's a whole range of other activities worth considering as well. What's more, operators and rental outlets in Waikīkī and all over the island are ready and waiting to provide any equipment or instruction you may need.

▲ Atlantis submarine

Spend an amazing hour under the ocean, coming face to face with sharks and turtles – and you needn't even get your feet wet.

P.185 ▸ ESSENTIALS

▲ Kayaking at Kailua Beach

With its placid turquoise waters, gorgeous Kailua Beach is the ideal spot to rent a kayak and escape the crowds.

P.131 ▸ WINDWARD OAHU

▲ Boogie-boarding at Sandy Beach

So long as you know what you're doing, boogie-boarding in the relentless shorebreak at Sandy Beach is an exhilarating experience.

P.124 ▸ SOUTHEAST OAHU

▼ Outrigger canoe ride at Waikīkī Beach

An outrigger canoe ride gives you (almost) all the fun of surfing with (almost) none of the effort.

P.48 ▸ WAIKĪKĪ

▶ Snorkeling at Hanauma Bay

Tear yourself away from Waikīkī for half a day, and get one-on-one with the colorful tropical fish of Hanauma Bay Nature Preserve.

P.122 ▸ SOUTHEAST OAHU

Hawaiiana

Even if you spend your whole vacation in Waikīkī, you're not just anywhere in the world – you're in Hawaii. And when you're in Hawaii, you do as the Hawaiians do – get yourself some *aloha* wear, learn to say "*mahalo*" rather than "thank you," bedeck yourself in flowery *leis*, and dance the *hula* at a *lū'au*. You won't regret a moment of it.

▲ Tiki souvenirs

Before you go home, be sure to pick up a few *hula* dolls, *tiki* carvings, and swizzle sticks for that Hawaiian theme bar you've decided to build in your basement.

P.188 ▶ ESSENTIALS

▼ Leis

From the moment you get your first *lei*, you'll be hooked – and Chinatown is the place to feed your new addiction.

P.189 ▶ ESSENTIALS

▼ Bob's Ukulele Store

Whether you see yourself as a budding Elvis or Eddie Kamae, or even just Tiny Tim, Bob's the man to sort you out with your first ukulele.

P.52 ▶ WAIKĪKĪ

▲ Lū'aus

Sadly none of Oahu's commercial lū'aus really matches up to the romantic image of an all-singing, all-dancing, all-night Hawaiian beach party, but after a cocktail or two on Waikīkī Beach you probably won't care.

P.182 ▶ ESSENTIALS

▼ Aloha shirts

Almost everyone in Hawaii – not just the tourists – really does wear colorful *aloha* shirts. Before you know it, you'll be buying some too.

P.189 ▶ ESSENTIALS

Places

Waikīkī

On any one day, half of all the tourists in the state of Hawaii are crammed into the tiny, surreal enclave of Waikīkī, three miles east of downtown Honolulu. Once this was a favored residence of the chiefs of Oahu; since its first hotel, the *Moana*, went up in 1901, it has mushroomed beyond belief. Its incredible profusion of skyscrapers hold enough hotel rooms to accommodate more than 100,000 guests, as well as hundreds of restaurants and stores. Waikīkī's natural setting is just as beguiling as its melee of activity. Off to the east, the sharp profile of Diamond Head rises up from the ocean, while the lush green Koʻolau mountains soar inland. In the evening especially, as the orange sun sinks far out to sea, the effect is magical.

Central Waikīkī Beach

The center of Waikīkī Beach is generally considered to extend from the area near Duke Kahanamoku's statue (see p.49) where the buildings on the ocean side of Kalākaua Avenue come to a halt, and the sidewalk turns into a beachfront promenade. Swimmers here enjoy the best conditions of the entire seafront, with softly shelving sands, and waters that are generally calm.

With so many visitors eager to sample Hawaii's signature watersports, this is also the prime spot for commercial activity operators. Several concession stands rent out surfboards, typically for $10 per hour, and offer surfing lessons

▼ WAIKĪKĪ BEACH

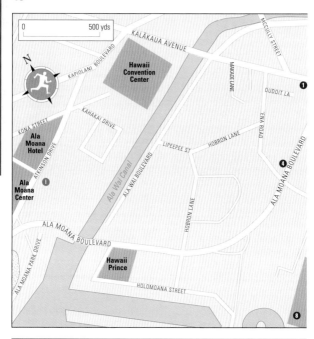

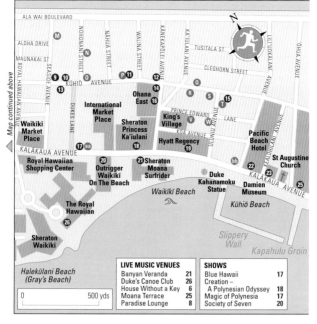

LIVE MUSIC VENUES		SHOWS	
Banyan Veranda	21	Blue Hawaii	17
Duke's Canoe Club	26	Creation –	
House Without a Key	6	A Polynesian Odyssey	18
Moana Terrace	25	Magic of Polynesia	17
Paradise Lounge	8	Society of Seven	20

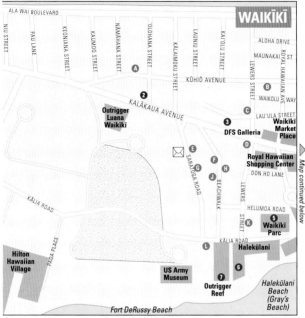

Map continued below

RESTAURANTS AND CAFÉS	
Banyan Veranda	21
Cheeseburger in Paradise	23
Ciao Mein	19
The Colony	19
Daily Buzz	16
Duke's Canoe Club	26
Eggs 'n' Things	1
Golden Dragon	8
Honolulu Coffee Co	21
House Without a Key	6
Keo's in Waikīkī	14
Nick's Fishmarket	2
Nobu	5
Oceanarium	22
Orchids	6
Perry's Smorgy	12
Ruffage Natural Foods	15
Sansei Seafood Restaurant & Sushi Bar	25
Shore Bird Beach Broiler	7
Singha Thai Cuisine	4
Todai Seafood Buffet	4

ACCOMMODATION	
Aloha Punawai	E
Aqua Bamboo & Spa	Q
Aqua Continental	R
Aqua Island Colony	M
The Breakers	J
Cabana at Waikīkī	U
Central Branch YMCA	I
Hale Aloha Hostel (Hostelling International Waikīkī)	V
Hawaiian King	N
Hawaiiana Hotel	F
Ilima Hotel	O
Imperial of Waikīkī	K
Kai Aloha	G
Ohana Islander Waikīkī	D
Ohana Maile Sky Court	A
Ohana Waikīkī Beachcomber	aa
Ohana Waikīkī Malia	B
Ohana Waikīkī West	P
Outrigger Regency on Beachwalk	H
Outrigger Waikīkī Shore	L
Pacific Ohana	X
Polynesian Hostel Beach Club	Z
ResortQuest Pacific Monarch	S
ResortQuest Waikīkī Circle Hotel	bb
ResortQuest Waikīkī Joy	C
Royal Grove	T
Waikīkī Beachside Hotel & Hostel	Y
Waikīkī Prince	W

BARS AND CLUBS	
Angles Waikīkī	9
Fusion	10
Hula's Bar and Lei Stand	24
In-Between	3
Lewers Lounge	6
Nashville Waikīkī	11
Zanzabar	13

▲ OUTRIGGER CANOE

for beginners at around $40 per hour, with prices ranging upwards if you want a solo lesson. You can also take a $10 ride in a colorful, traditional outrigger canoe, paddled by experts – it's a similarly exhilarating experience to surfing, but requires far less effort.

Royal-Moana Beach

To the west, central Waikīkī Beach merges into Royal-Moana Beach, fronting the *Royal Hawaiian* and *Sheraton Moana* hotels. It can sometimes be a struggle to walk along this narrow, busy strip because of the crowds it draws, but the swimming here is, again, excellent. It's also ideal for novice surfers: head slightly to the right as you enter the water to reach the easy break known as Canoes' Surf (so called because these gentle waves were all the heavy old *koa* canoes could ride). The waves are a bit stronger further left, at the Queen's Surf break.

Halekūlani Beach

West of the *Royal Hawaiian*, a raised walkway curves in front of the *Sheraton Waikīkī*, where the sea comes right over the sand. After a tiny little "pocket beach," a long straight walkway squeezes between the waves and the grand *Halekūlani Hotel*. At the far end comes a slightly larger stretch of beach, known as Halekūlani Beach or, alternatively, Gray's Beach. To the ancient Hawaiians it was renowned as Kawehewehe, a place where the waters were said to have special healing properties. It too is a popular swimming spot, though erosion in recent years has scoured away much of the sand on the sea bed, so reef shoes are advisable.

Fort DeRussy Beach

Beyond Gray's Beach, the sands grow broader as you pass in front of the military base and the *Hale Koa* hotel, which although it's reserved for military personnel has a beachfront bar that's open to all customers. The walking can be a bit slow on the thick sand of Fort DeRussy Beach itself, but it's backed by some pleasant lawns and an open pavilion naturally sheltered by interlaced trees. Concessions stands here rent out surf and boogie boards, along with huge, garish pedalos. Few people swim at this point, however, as the ocean floor is sharp and rocky.

Kahanamoku Beach

Kahanamoku Beach, the westernmost section of the Waikīkī shorefront, Kahanamoku Beach, flanks the *Hilton Hawaiian Village* (reviewed on p.170). Duke Kahanamoku's grandfather was granted most of the twenty-acre plot on which the hotel now stands in the Great Mahele of 1848. Thanks to its carefully sculpted shelf of sand, the beach where Duke was raised is ideal for family bathing, but it somehow lacks the concentrated glamor or excitement of central Waikīkī.

Kūhiō Beach

Kūhiō Beach, which runs east from central Waikīkī, is one of Waikīkī's busiest areas. The protective walls and breakwaters that jut into the ocean here shelter two separate lagoons where swimming is safe and comfortable. The easternmost wall, the Kapahulu Groin, projects well above the waterline, and makes a good vantage point for photos of the Waikīkī panorama. On the other hand, the long, seaweed-covered Slippery Wall, parallel to the beach roughly fifty yards out, is washed over by every wave. Daredevil locals boogie-board just outside the wall, but the currents are so strong that you should only join them if you really know what you're doing.

At 6pm every night, a conch shell blows to signal the start of a free hula show on the lawns beside Kūhiō Beach. With island musicians and dancers performing by the light of flaming torches, it's a perfect way to relax at sunset, at the end of another long, hard day.

The Duke Kahanamoku statue

The logical place to start a walking tour of Waikīkī is in the middle of Waikīkī Beach,

▼ SLIPPERY WALL

▲ SUNSET ON WAIKĪKĪ BEACH

on seafront Kalākaua Avenue, where a statue of Duke Kahanamoku (1890–1968) is always wreathed in *leis*. The archetypal "Beach Boy," Duke represented the US in three Olympics, winning swimming golds in both 1912 and 1920. His subsequent exhibition tours popularized the Hawaiian art of surfing all over the world,

▼ DUKE KAHANAMOKU STATUE

and as Sheriff of Honolulu he continued to welcome celebrity visitors to Hawaii until his death in 1968. Sadly, the statue stands with its back to the ocean, a pose Duke seldom adopted in life; otherwise he'd be gazing at the spot where in 1917 he rode a single 35-foot wave a record total of one and a quarter miles.

The Sheraton Moana Surfrider and the Royal Hawaiian

Just west of the Duke Kahanamoku statue, the wedge-like shape of the *Sheraton Moana Surfrider* forces Kalākaua Avenue away from the ocean. Though not Waikīkī's first hotel, the *Moana* is the oldest still standing, and has been transformed back to a close approximation of its original 1901 appearance. The luxurious settees of its long Beaux Arts lobby make an ideal spot to catch up with the newspapers.

Further west from there, where once swayed the ten-thousand-strong royal Helumoa coconut grove – of which a few palms still survive – the beachfront here is today dominated by the *Royal Hawaiian Hotel*, also known as the "Pink

Palace." Its Spanish-Moorish architecture was all the rage when it opened in 1927, with a room rate of $14 per night, but its grandeur is now somewhat swamped by a towering new wing.

Waikīkī Beach Walk

The area to the west of the *Royal Hawaiian* has been the focus over the last few years of a huge redevelopment project, spearheaded by the Outrigger group of hotels, under the overall name of Waikīkī Beach Walk. So far, it amounts to little more than the turning of what was previously a rather run-down couple of blocks along Lewers Street, stretching towards the sea, into a sort of glitzy annex of the upscale end of Kalākaua Avenue. At the time of writing, a couple of high-end new hotels were set to open, as well as restaurants including a branch of Roy's (see p.127), but no big-name retailers had yet announced plans to open stores here. Major changes are more likely to follow the opening of the much-trumpeted *Trump International Hotel*, a 350-foot hotel and condo development currently scheduled to open in 2009. Even before ground was broken on that project, in 2006, every condo in the building was sold on the largest first-day sale in history.

▲ ROYAL HAWAIIAN HOTEL

The US Army Museum

Tues–Sun 10am–4.15pm; free. On maps, the military base of Fort DeRussy, at the western edge of Waikīkī, looks like a welcome expanse of green. In fact, it's largely taken up by parking lots and tennis courts, and is not a place to stroll for pleasure. At its oceanfront side, however, the US Army Museum is located in a low concrete structure which, as Battery Randolph, housed massive artillery pieces that were directed by observers stationed atop Diamond Head during World War II. Displays here trace the history of warfare in Hawaii back to the time of Kamehameha the Great, with the bulk of the collection consisting of the various guns and cannons that have been used

▲ TANK AT THE US ARMY MUSEUM

to defend Honolulu since the US Army first arrived, four days after annexation in 1898.

The Damien Museum

130 Ohua Ave. ☎808/923-2690 Mon–Fri 9am–3pm; free. Father Damien, the nineteenth-century Belgian priest who ranks among Hawaii's greatest heroes, is commemorated in the simple Damien Museum, not far east from the Duke Kahanamoku statue. This unobtrusive shrine sits beneath a schoolroom behind the angular modern Catholic church of St Augustine. Damien's life and work is evoked by an assortment of mundane items, such as receipts for cases of soda and barrels of flour, and his prayer books and vestments. Although he established churches all over Hawaii, Damien's fame derives principally from his final sojourn in the leper colony at Kalaupapa on the island of Molokai. He eventually succumbed to the disease himself on April 15, 1889, at the age of 49; harrowing deathbed photos show the ravages it inflicted on him.

Shops

Bob's Ukulele Store

Waikīkī Beach Marriott, 2552 Kalākaua Ave ☎808/921-5365, ⓦwww .bobsukulele.com. Daily 9am–noon & 5–9.30pm. Strewn with a rich canopy of beautifully crafted ukuleles, Bob's offers the best range of instruments in the city, along with koa hardwood gifts, songbooks, and a fine selection of Hawaiian CDs.

Borders Express

Waikīkī Marketplace, 2250 Kalākaua Ave ☎808/922-4154. Daily 9.30am–9.30pm. In the bookstore desert that is Waikīkī, this mini Borders branch, hidden away on the third floor of the otherwise tacky and unappealing Waikīkī Marketplace mall, is a life-saver. Come here for a good range of Hawaiiana, along with novels, travel books, and useful maps.

Cina Cina

Royal Hawaiian Hotel, 2259 Kalākaua Ave ☎808/926-0444, ⓦwww .cinacinahawaii.com. Daily 9am–9pm. Pan-Asian style is given a quirky twist in this elegant women's store, with jewelry, fans, incense, purses, clothes, and cards, plus a small range of home accessories.

Cinnamon Girl

Sheraton Moana Surfrider Hotel, 2365 Kalākaua Ave ☎808/922-5336, ⓦwww.cinnamongirl.com. Daily 9am–10pm. Fresh, feminine, and funky, the fusion of youthful island fashion with shabby chic is a successful one. This small homegrown chain is best known for its pretty dresses and children's clothes, designed and made in Hawaii, but also offers gorgeous gifts, cards, purses, ceramics, flip flops, and bath and beauty products.

Further branches located in the Ala Moana Center (see p.91) and Ward Warehouse (see p.92) malls.

DFS Galleria

330 Royal Hawaiian Ave at Kalākaua Ave ☎808/931-2655, ⓦwww .dfsgalleria.com. Daily 9am–11pm. Much beloved by Japanese tourists, who flock here on organized tours and on regular shuttle buses from major hotels, the compact Galleria offers an all-in-one souvenir-buying experience. The ground floor is taken up by aloha wear and Hawaiian gifts – chocolate-coated mac nuts, pineapple-shaped toothpick holders, and hibiscus-strewn ukuleles (some of which can be found cheaper in the ABC stores). The flight above is the preserve of chains like DKNY and Guess, while the third-floor, an exclusive Duty Free enclave accessible only with an international air ticket, features big-hitters like Loewe, Hermes, Bulgari, and Prada.

Gallery Tokusa

Halekūlani Hotel, 2199 Kalia Rd ☎808/926-1766. Daily 9am–9pm. Gallery Tokusa maintains the

Halekūlani's elegant tone with its exquisite range of Japanese decorative arts, including silk fans, ivory metsuke, Hawaiian ox-bone carvings, and beautifully crafted antique imari. Prices are high, though they do have an affordable range of funky jewelry made from semi-precious stones.

Honolua Surf Co

Outrigger Waikīkī, 2335 Kalākaua Ave ☎808/926-4814, ⓦhonoluasurf.com. Daily 9am–9pm. Cut-above surfwear-influenced clothing – mostly for men, but with some funky styles for women, too – with an urban edge. Other branches around town, including in the Aloha Tower Marketplace (see p.92).

International Marketplace

2330 Kalākaua Ave ☎808/971-2080, ⓦwww.internationalmarketplaceWaikīkī. com. Daily 10am–10.30pm. For the moment, this rambling open-air complex survives, though encroaching development may soon force its closure. Slightly down-at-heel and a little disheveled, its wooden carts – selling everything from sunglasses to pearls in oyster shells – scattered among the mighty banyan trees, it has more atmosphere than the shiny new malls, though the tatty "crafts" on sale tend to be made in Taiwan, and the "psychic readers" are as a rule devoid of paranormal powers. There's a cybercafé, *WikiWiki*, 2301 Kūhiō Ave (☎808/923-9797; Mon–Sat 10am–10pm, Sun noon–10pm), along with a convenient little food court area – complete with sushi bar – where you can hear live Hawaiian music five nights a week.

King's Village

131 Kaiulani Ave ⓦwww.kings-village .com. Daily 9am–11pm. Compact open-air mall where the spurious,

▲ SOUVENIRS, INTERNATIONAL MARKETPLACE

vaguely regal theme (there's a changing of the guard ceremony nightly at 6.15pm) and location, slightly off the main road, gives it an air of pretension absent at the unabashedly touristy International Marketplace. With its cobblestone paths, plantation-style architecture, and abundant greenery, it's pleasant enough for a quick browse, though few stores – other than a handful of resort wear outlets and local arts and crafts vendors – hold much interest. On the second floor, the tranquil Taiwanese tea house *Cha No Ma* makes for a peaceful spot to refuel.

Martin and Macarthur

Hyatt Regency Waikīkī, 2424 Kalākaua Ave ☎808/923-5333, ⓦwww .martinandmacarthur.com. Daily 9am– 11am. Also in the Ala Moana Center (see p.91). Dark and sleek handcrafted koa hardwood furniture, perfect for kitting your house out with island style – at a price.

Pipe Dreams Surf Co

270 Lewers St ☎808/923-2681, ⓦwww.pipedreamssurfco.com. Also a branch in Aloha Tower Marketplace (see p.92). Daily 9am–10pm. One of Hawaii's better surfwear stores, with eye-catching aloha shirts – including some by designer Tori Richard – and Quiksilver surfing gear, along with surfboards, skateboards, and inexpensive, funky jewelry made from painted *kokua* nuts.

Royal Hawaiian Shopping Center

2201 Kalākaua Ave ☎808/922-0588, ⓦwww.shopwaikiki.com. Daily 10am–10pm. Sprawling across three full blocks, the Royal Hawaiian dominates Waikīkī's mall scene – though it has fewer actual places to shop than you might imagine. Centering on a coconut grove, its anchor stores include Bulgari, Fendi, and Hermès, along with Juicy Couture. Daily hula, *lei*-making, and ukulele classes are available.

Tori Richard

Hyatt Regency Waikīkī, 2424 Kalākaua Ave ☎808/924-1811, ⓦwww .toririchard.com. Daily 9am–11am. Also in the Ala Moana Center (see p.91). Since 1956 the Tori Richard brand has been taking the aloha shirt onto a different level, creating artistic, classy shirts with subtle, retro and often whimsical designs, in fine silk and linen. The womenswear range, though it features bold prints and gorgeous colors, has less of an edge. Prices aren't low – but then this isn't your standard viscose resort wear.

Cafés

Daily Buzz

Ohana East, 150 Kaiulani Ave ☎808/922-2223. Daily 6am–2pm.
Tucked away off the main lobby of the *Ohana East* hotel, this convenient, slightly faded coffee corner offers good espresso drinks, cooked breakfasts, sandwiches and bagels, plus Internet access ($4/hr, or all-in-one coffee/pastry/Web access deals). The quirky attempts at *tiki* styling don't add much atmosphere, but it's a friendly spot.

Honolulu Coffee Co

Sheraton Moana Surfrider, 2365 Kalākaua Ave ☎808/533-1500. Daily 6am–10pm. Tucked away in one of Waikīkī's most appealing old hotels, this soothing, airy spot continues the *Moana Surfrider's* understated island/colonial decor, with huge open windows, tongue-and-groove paneling, and simple darkwood furniture. The exquisite patisserie – including a creamy "green tearamisu", shaped like a tea cup and dusted with green tea – makes a great accompaniment for expertly made espresso drinks and freshly ground Kona coffee.

Restaurants

Banyan Veranda

Sheraton Moana Surfrider, 2365 Kalākaua Ave ☎808/921-4600. Mon–Sat 7–11am, 1–4pm & 5.30–9pm; Sun 9am–1pm, 3–4pm & 5.30–9pm.
Fancy restaurant in one of Waikīkī's most atmospheric old hotels. Full "sunrise" ($29) or Japanese-style ($31) breakfasts are available, along with à la carte choices, daily except Sunday, when the lavish brunch costs $45. Instead of lunch, they serve an elaborate afternoon tea, which has become quite a Waikīkī tradition: $29.50 buys a plate of finger sandwiches and pastries and a pot of tea to be enjoyed as you listen to a Hawaiian guitarist, while for $35 you get a couple of glasses of fizz too. A four-course prix-fixe dinner (5.30–9pm) costs $57.50 (you can also go à la carte, with entrees like *onaga* for around $35); your meal is accompanied by live Hawaiian music and, occasionally, the shrieks of noisy revelers in the beachfront bar.

Cheeseburger in Paradise

2500 Kalākaua Ave ☎808/923-3731. Daily 7am–midnight. The Waikīkī outlet of this successful Maui burger joint occupies a prime position, across the street from the ocean, with airy open windows and retro 1950s *tiki/* beachcomber style. The food, however, is nothing to write home about – best go for the cheeseburgers over the salads.

Ciao Mein

Hyatt Regency Waikīkī, 2424 Kalākaua Ave ☎808/923-2426. Daily 6–10pm. Huge restaurant serving an odd but successful mixture of Chinese and Italian cuisine. Not all dishes actually combine the two, though "Collision Cuisine" specials at around $24 include "Hot Bean Salmon alla Siciliana" and seafood lasagne. There's a tasty focaccia appetizer for $9, and most pasta entrees cost $19. Chinese entrees include sizzling Mongolian beef and honey walnut shrimp (both $26), and there are vegetarian options, too.

The Colony

Hyatt Regency Waikīkī, 2424 Kalākaua Ave ☎808/923-1234. Daily 5–10pm. Appetizers at this, the grandest, most formal and most traditionally American of the *Hyatt's* restaurants, include a three-onion soup for $8. Steaks, which cost from $35, are the specialty here, grilled over kiawe wood and available in all sorts of combinations (steak with lobster is $72); you can also get a delicious fresh catch for $28, or a "Hukilau" of steamed seafood for two or more at $32 per person. Most diners set the ball rolling with one of the restaurant's award-winning martinis, and it's the done thing to save space for the Chocolate in Paradise dessert – sixteen layers of chocolate cake bliss.

Duke's Canoe Club

Outrigger Waikīkī, 2335 Kalākaua Ave ☎808/922-2268, 🅦www .dukeswaikiki.com. Daily 6.30am–midnight. Right on the beach, with an open-air *lānai*, this crowded, lively place (a small Hawaiian/Californian chain) offers not only great views of the waves but also a feast of retro *tiki* and surf styling, with vintage photos and memorabilia tastefully set around the jungle hut decor. The buffet breakfasts (until 10.30am), which include hot items, are not bad value at $14.95, but for lunch it's best to ignore the buffet ($12.95) in favor of the *pupu* menu, which includes large plates of scrumptious crab-and-macadamia nut wontons ($9). At night, there's a full (if unimaginative) dinner menu, with chicken, steak, and fish entrees at around $20. Big-name Hawaiian musicians play Fri–Sun 4–6pm.

Eggs 'n' Things

1911B Kalākaua Ave ☎808/949-0820. Daily 11pm–2pm. All-night diner and local institution, drawing a big breakfast crowd – surfers, night workers, bright-eyed tourists – for its bargain omelets, waffles, and crepes. The Early Riser (5–9am) and Late Riser (1–2pm & 1–2am) specials give you three pancakes and two eggs for just $4.25. No reservations, so expect a wait.

Golden Dragon

Hilton Hawaiian Village, 2005 Kālia Rd ☎808/946-5336. Daily except Mon 6–9.30pm. The classiest Chinese restaurant in Waikīkī, with garden seating overlooking a lagoon, and a tasteful indoor dining room. The food is good, and prices not as high as you might expect, with entrees such as crispy lemon chicken, roast duck, and noodles with fish or chicken starting at around $17. Seafood dishes – seared ocean scallops, Kung Pao shrimp, opakapaka in black bean sauce – cost a little more, while a tempting range of set menus cost between $34 per person for a healthy selection to $55 per person for the elaborate "Chrysanthemum Dinner".

House Without a Key

Halekūlani, 2199 Kālia Rd ☎808/923-2311. Daily 7am–9pm. Waikīkī Beach's loveliest venue for an open-air sunset cocktail – complete with top-quality live Hawaiian music (see p.60) – is an elegant, understated spot, with a far less frenetic atmosphere than the other oceanfront places, and gorgeous views from every table. The food is tasty and relatively simple, and especially good value in the evening. At lunch *saimin* goes for $13, while a chicken and sage-roasted apple salad is $17; the dinner menu features lots of *pupus*, including a combination platter of coconut shrimp, lemongrass beef skewers and seafood spring roll for $16.50.

Keo's in Waikiki

2028 Kūhiō Ave ☎808/951-9355, ⓦwww.keosthaicuisine.com. Sun–Thurs 7am–2pm & 5–10.30pm, Fri & Sat 7am–2pm & 5–11pm. Keo's has long proclaimed itself to be Hawaii's best Thai restaurant, and its walls are festooned with photos of celebrities enticed by trademark dishes such as the "Evil Jungle Prince" curry. There's no disputing that the food tastes good, and with all entrees except the very fanciest seafood options costing under $16, prices are reasonable. Breakfast is both American and Asian; lunch and dinner are entirely Thai. There's another branch, *Keoni by Keo's*, at 2375 Kūhiō Ave.

Nick's Fishmarket

Waikīkī Gateway Hotel, 2070 Kalākaua Ave ☎808/955-6333, ⓦwww.nicksfishmarket.com. Mon–Thurs & Sun 5.30–10pm, Fri & Sat 5.30–11pm. Fancy fish restaurant, with dark leatherette seating, glittering glass and mirrors, and a formal, romantic atmosphere. The cooking is not especially innovative, but the preparation is meticulous and the range of choices amazing. Appetizers,

priced $12–18, include coconut shrimp and oysters Rockefeller. A typical main dish like Hawaiian swordfish costs around $30, a mixed seafood grill $42, and lobsters up to $75. Simpler *pupus* served until midnight nightly in the less formal adjoining lounge, which also has live music.

Nobu

Waikīkī Parc, 2233 Helumoa Rd ☎808/921-7272, ⓦwww.nobumatsuhisa.com. This book went to press just before the eagerly awaited opening of the first Hawaiian outpost of Japanese-Peruvian chef Nobu Matsuhisa's empire, spreading outdoors from the *Parc's* ultra-smart lobby. Expect exquisite, and expensive, sushi, sashimi, and "special cold dishes," with set dinners starting at around $30 for a sashimi platter with appetizers, soup and rice, or $80 and up for the chef's tasting menu.

Oceanarium

Pacific Beach Hotel, 2490 Kalākaua Ave ☎808/922-6111. Daily 6am–10pm. Functionally furnished restaurant with one big gimmick – one wall of the dining room is a three-storey aquarium, so as you eat your meal you can watch (and be watched by) four hundred live fish, plus the occasional scuba

▼ OCEANARIUM

diver. The day starts with a continental breakfast (6–11am) for $11 or a $16 buffet. Lunchtime noodles, burgers, salads, or sandwiches all cost around $12, while for dinner you can either go for a $32 prime rib and seafood buffet, or order individual meat or fish entrees for around $20.

Orchids

Halekūlani, 2199 Kālia Rd ☎808/923-2311. Mon–Sat 7.30–11am, 11.30am–2pm & 6–10pm, Sun 9.30am–2.30pm & 6–10pm. Creative, contemporary seafood restaurant, a minimal space afroth with orchids in the classiest hotel on Waikīkī Beach, that's well worth splashing out for. Set in a divine spot, open to the ocean and affording panoramic views of Diamond Head, it offers a perfect combination of elegance and relaxation (though note there are no shorts, T-shirts or sandals allowed in the evening). The food, fusing Asian and island cooking, is outstanding, if pricey – you can get a Madras seafood curry at lunch for $21, but it's most romantic at night, when entrées like *ahi*-seared sashimi with spices, *moi* with hearts of palm, and steamed *onaga* start at $30.The elaborate Sunday brunch is a local favorite for special occasions.

Perry's Smorgy

2380 Kūhiō Ave ☎808/926-0184, ⓦwww.perryssmorgy.com. Daily 7–11am, 11.30am–2.30pm & 5–9pm; Sun brunch 11.30am–2.30pm. All-you-can-eat buffets, served indoors or in a Japanese-style garden. The food neither looks edible nor tastes of anything much but the place is always crowded with bargain-hunters. Choose from the $6.95 breakfast (ham, beef hash, sausages, pancakes, pastries,

juices), the $7.95 lunch (mahimahi, Southern fried chicken, garlic bread, rice, baked macaroni, desserts), the $10.95 dinner (beef, shrimp, ribs, turkey, teriyaki chicken), or the $10.95 Sunday brunch.

Ruffage Natural Foods

2443 Kūhiō Ave ☎808/922-2042. Mon–Sat 9am–6pm. Tiny whole food grocery with a takeout counter and limited patio seating. The selection is great, with granola breakfasts and delicious real-fruit and honey smoothies; avocado and bean-sprout sandwiches and vegan burritos; and salads, pasta, and tofu dishes. Most things cost less than $7. From 6pm to midnight the front section transforms into an inexpensive sushi bar.

Sansei Seafood Restaurant & Sushi Bar

Waikīkī Beach Marriott Resort & Spa, 2552 Kalākaua Ave ☎808/931-6286, ⓦwww.sanseihawaii.com. Daily 5.30–10pm; late-night sushi Fri & Sat until 2am. The food at this buzzing local favorite is outstanding, and very well priced, whether you go for the full Pacific Rim menu or stick to the sushi bar. Best of all, the $68 "Omakase" tasting menu for two is an amazing bargain, giving a beautifully balanced feast of seafood, sushi and sashimi. A la carte sushi starts at $5 (try the fruity mango crab salad roll, or the Sansei Special, with spicy crab, cilantro, cucumber, and avocado, dusted with *furikake* and served with a sweet *Thai chili* sauce), while appetizers ($3–11) include a delicious panko-crusted ahi sashimi. Entrees like grilled *opah* over fresh nalo greens, roasted Japanese jerk chicken, or duck breast in a foie gras demi glaze, are between $18 and $40. The adjoining karaoke bar gets going when the restaurant closes, with a limited half-price appetizer and sushi menu.

Shore Bird Beach Broiler

Outrigger Reef, 2169 Kalia Rd ☎808/922-2887. Daily 7–11am & 4.30–10pm. Perennially popular, cheap-and-cheerful open-air hotel restaurant, right on the beach, where the sumptuous views – if you're lucky enough to get a prime oceanfront table – and the crashing waves make up for the less than inspiring food. The breakfast buffet costs $12, while dinner with an open salad bar is $18–23, depending on your choice of entree. Guests can cook their own meat or fish at a communal grill; kids adore it.

Singha Thai Cuisine

1910 Ala Moana Blvd ☎808/941-2898, ⊛www.singhathai.com. Daily 4–10pm. Bright, elegant, dinner-only place that serves delicious Thai food with a definite Hawaiian tinge, including fresh fish and scallop dishes ($20 and up), plus curries and pad Thai (both around $16), and hot-and-sour *tom yum* soups ($6). Signature entrees, including spicy Siamese fighting fish, cost $20–32. Thai dancers perform nightly 7–9pm.

Todai Seafood Buffet

1910 Ala Moana Blvd ☎808/947-1000, ⊛www.todai.com. Mon–Thurs 11.30am–2pm & 5.30–9.30pm, Fri 11.30am–2pm & 5–10pm, Sat 11.30am–2.30pm & 5–10pm, Sun 11am–2.30pm & 5–10pm. Large, bustling outlet of a superb upscale Japanese chain, in western Waikīkī. Lunch costs $15 (Mon–Fri) or $17 (Sat & Sun), while dinner is $27.95 (Mon–Thurs) or $28.95 (Fri–Sun); the range and quality of the food makes it a real bargain. Super-tasty seafood dishes at the 160-foot buffet bar include handmade sushi rolls, *ahi poke*, sashimi, shrimp, oysters, and scallops on the half-shell; cooked noodle dishes; teppanyaki, and chicken teriyaki and pork for diehard carnivores. Even the desserts are good.

Bars and clubs

Angles Waikīkī

2256 Kūhiō Ave ☎808/926-9766 or 923-1130, ⊛www.angleswaikiki.com. Daily 10am–2am. Gay dance club with lively bar and street-view patio, plus bar games including pool and darts.

Fusion

2260 Kūhiō Ave ☎808/924-2422, ⊛www.gayhawaii.com/fusion. Mon–Thurs 9pm–4am, Fri & Sat 8pm–4am, Sun 10pm–4am. Wild, split-level gay nightclub, with male strippers, drag acts, free karaoke Mon & Tues, and special drink discounts.

Hula's Bar and Lei Stand

Waikīkī Grand Hotel, 134 Kapahulu Ave ☎808/923-0669, ⊛www.hulas.com. Daily 10am–2am. Waikīkī's most popular and long-standing gay club occupies a suite of ocean-view rooms on the second floor of the *Waikīkī Grand*, across from the Honolulu Zoo. In addition to a state-of-the-art dance bar equipped with giant video screens, there's a more casual lounge area. No cover.

In-Between

2155 Lau'ula St ☎808/926-7060, ⊛www.inbetweenonline.com. Mon–Sat 4pm–2am, Sun 2pm–2am. Local gay karaoke bar with an extensive song list and daily drink specials located in the heart of Waikīkī.

Lewers Lounge

Halekūlani, 2199 Kālia Rd ☎808/923-2311. Daily 5pm until late.

▲ HOUSE WITHOUT A KEY

Sophisticated hotel nightspot that looks more like an English drawing room than a Waikīkī bar. Live jazz nightly 8.30pm–12.30am, at its best Tues–Fri, when bass player Bruce Hamada performs.

Nashville Waikīkī

2330 Kūhiō Ave ☎ 808/926-7911, Ⓦ www.nashvillewaikiki.com. Daily 4pm–4am. If you're hankering to hoedown in Hawaii, this country music club below the *Ohana West* has plenty of room to show off your rhinestones. Check ahead, though; it also hosts hip-hop and DJ nights. There are pool tables and darts, too.

Zanzabar

World Trade Center, 2255 Kūhiō Ave ☎ 808/924-3939, Ⓦ www .zanzabarhawaii.com. Nightly except Mon 8pm–4am. Extremely opulent nightclub, bursting with Egyptian motifs, and pumping out dance music to the well-heeled youth of Honolulu. Cover varies.

Live music venues

Beach Bar

Sheraton Moana Surfrider, 2365 Kalākaua Ave ☎ 808/922-3111. Open-air beach bar that was home to the nationally syndicated Hawaii Calls radio show from the 1930s to the 1970s. Steel guitar and hula dancers nightly 5.30–7.30pm, followed by small Hawaiian ensembles 7.30–10.30pm. No cover but a one-drink minimum.

Duke's Canoe Club

Outrigger Waikīkī, 2335 Kalākaua Ave ☎ 808/922-2268. Smooth Hawaiian sounds wash over this oceanfront cocktail bar nightly from 4–6pm and 10pm–midnight. On weekends, the afternoon show is usually a big-name "Concert on the Beach." No cover charge.

House Without a Key

Halekūlani, 2199 Kālia Rd ☎ 808/923-2311. This very romantic, very spacious beach bar was named after a Charlie Chan mystery that was written by Earl Derr Biggers after a stay at the hotel. In keeping with its name, the *House Without a Key* barely has walls, let alone a door, which affords it the most wonderful vistas, and most nights it's blessed with spectacular ocean sunsets. The evening cocktail hour (5–9pm) is an unmissable bargain, with very gentle, old-time Hawaiian classics performed under an ancient *kiawe* tree by top-notch musicians, and hula dancing by a former Miss Hawaii (two of whom alternate). You're led to your seats, which avoids the scrum for an oceanfront spot at other beach bars; and in any case you're practically guaranteed a sea view from every table. Drinks prices are low, given the quality of the experience, and service is friendly and courteous. No cover.

Moana Terrace

Waikīkī Beach Marriott, 2552 Kalākaua Ave ☏808/922-6611. A consistently good roster of Hawaiian musicians perform at this lively, open-air, third-story cocktail bar, across the road from the beach, Mon–Wed, Fri & Sat from 7pm, and Sun from 8pm. The biggest treat of all comes on Thursdays, when local legend Auntie Genoa Keawe, a magnificent falsetto singer now approaching her ninetieth birthday, leads an informal jam session 6–8.30pm. No cover.

Paradise Lounge

Hilton Hawaiian Village, 2005 Kālia Rd ☏808/949-4321. Live hula and Hawaiian music, headlined by popular local group Olomana, Fri & Sat 8pm–midnight. No cover.

Shows

Blue Hawaii

Waikīkī Beachcomber Hotel, 2300 Kalākaua Ave ☏808/923-1245, ⓦwww.bluehawaiishow.com. Nightly except Mon 6.15pm. $70 with dinner; $42 show only. The one and only Jonathan von Brana, along with a perky troupe of dancing girls, evokes the spirit of Elvis in a musical tribute that takes him from the beaches of Hawaii to the stage of the *Las Vegas Hilton*. Some of his moves might seem a little incongruous – jumping jacks? – but he doles out enough scarves and teddy bears to keep the fans in a state of feverish

excitement. High-energy support is provided by the Love Notes, a doo-wop group who've been around the block a few times.

Creation – A Polynesian Odyssey

Ainahau Showroom, *Sheraton Princess Ka'iulani*, 120 Ka'iulani Ave ☏808/931-4660. Tues & Thurs–Sun 6pm. $68 with dinner; $38 show only. Lavish Polynesian revue, complete with fire-dancing, hula, and a buffet dinner.

Magic of Polynesia

Waikīkī Beachcomber Hotel, 2300 Kalākaua Ave ☏808/971-4321, ⓦwww.magicofpolynesia.com. Two shows nightly at 5pm & 8pm. $80 with dinner; $50 show only. Spectacular, enjoyable magic show, starring illusionists John Hirakawa (Tues–Sat) or Michael Villoria (Sun & Mon), which features all the disappearing lovelies and severed heads you could ask for, along with tattooed Polynesian warriors, maidens in coconut bras, and Samoan fire dancers.

Royal Hawaiian Lū'au

Royal Hawaiian Hotel, 2259 Kalākaua Ave ☏808/921-4600. Adults $99, ages 5–12 $55. Mon 6pm. Waikīkī Beach makes a wonderfully romantic setting for a *lū'au*, this one is expensive, but the price includes a reasonable spread of food and a cramped but enthusiastic show of Hawaiian music and dance on the oceanfront stage.

Society of Seven

Outrigger Main Show Room, 2335 Kalākaua Ave ☏808/922-6408, ⓦwww.outriggeractivities.com. Nightly except Mon 8.30pm. $52 with dinner; $37 show only. Very long-standing song-and-dance ensemble, which performs Broadway musical routines and pop hits with amazing energy.

Kapiʻolani Park and Diamond Head

The skyline to the east of Waikīkī is dominated by the craggy outer wall of Honolulu's most famous landmark, the eroded volcanic cinder cone of Diamond Head. However, that's still over a mile distant from Kapahulu Avenue, which marks the eastern limit of Waikīkī proper, and some very welcome green space lies in between in the appealing form of Kapiʻolani Park, home among other things to Honolulu Zoo. The adjoining oceanfront offers a similar respite from the frenzy of Waikīkī, with beaches that are generally much less crowded even though they're every bit as nice.

Kapahulu Avenue itself holds a number of interesting shops and restaurants, while inland from Diamond Head the Kahāla Mall is an upscale shopping center almost exclusively used by residents rather than tourists.

Kapiʻolani Park

Hawaii's first public park, Kapiʻolani Park, was established in 1877 by King David Kalākaua, and named for his queen. It originally held a number of ponds, until the completion of the Ala Wai Canal in 1928 cut off its supply of fresh water. Now locals flock to its open green lawns, with joggers pounding the footpaths, and practitioners of t'ai chi exercising in slow-motion beneath the banyans. The park was long the home of the kitsch Kodak Hula Show, but sadly that tradition has finally ended. However, the adjoining Waikīkī Shell hosts large concerts, especially in summer, while the Royal Hawaiian Band performs on the park's bandstand on Sundays at 2pm.

▼ ORANGUTAN AT HONOLULU ZOO

Honolulu Zoo

Kapiʻolani Park. Daily 9am–5.30pm, last admission 4.30pm; adults $8, ages 6–12 $1; ☏ 808/971-7171, ⓦ www.honoluluzoo.org. Honolulu Zoo occupies a verdant wedge on the fringes of Kapiʻolani Park, with its main entrance barely a minute's walk out from the bustle of Waikīkī. Sadly, it's all a bit too dilapidated and unkempt to be worth a thorough recommendation, and it's surprisingly hard to spot many

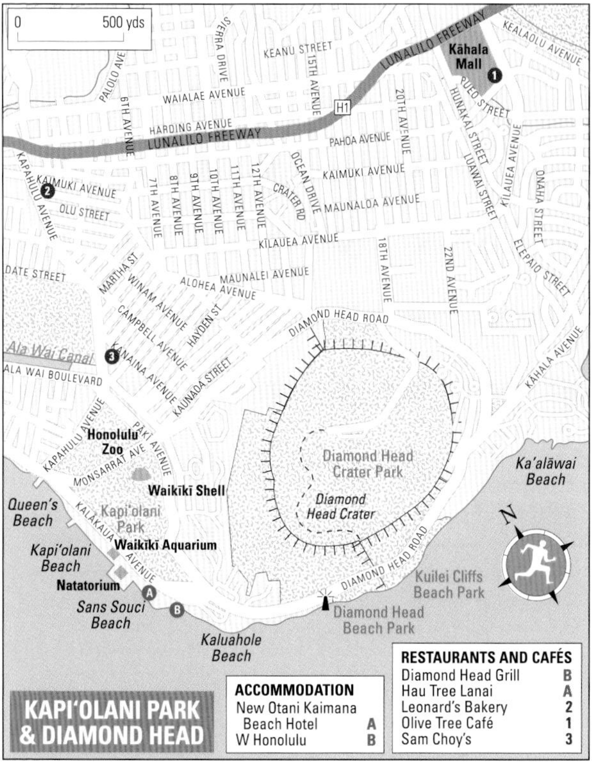

Map legend:

KAPIʻOLANI PARK & DIAMOND HEAD

ACCOMMODATION
New Otani Kaimana
 Beach Hotel — A
W Honolulu — B

RESTAURANTS AND CAFÉS
Diamond Head Grill — B
Hau Tree Lanai — A
Leonard's Bakery — 2
Olive Tree Café — 1
Sam Choy's — 3

of its animals in their ageing enclosures. On the positive side, the tropical undergrowth and blossoming trees can look pretty against the backdrop of Diamond Head, and kids may enjoy the chance to see species that range from wallowing hippos and gray kangaroos to unfortunate monkeys trapped on tiny islands in a crocodile-infested lagoon. The zoo's pride and joy, the African Savanna exhibit – a world of reddish mud where the "black" rhinos end up pretty much the color of their surroundings – is reasonably successful in re-creating the swamps and grasslands of Africa.

Kapiʻolani Park Beach

East of the Kapahulu Groin, at the end of the built-up section of Waikīkī, comes a gap in the beach where the sand all but disappears and the waters are not suitable for bathing. Not far beyond, however, to either side of the aquarium, Kapiʻolani Park Beach is a favorite with local families and fitness freaks, and is also known for having a strong gay presence. Banyans and coconut palms offer plenty of free shade and its lawns make a perfect picnic spot. Waikīkī's only substantial stretch of reasonably unspoiled coral reef runs a short distance offshore, shielding a pleasant, gentle swimming area.

The most used segment of the beach, nearest to Waikīkī, is Queen's Surf Beach Park – confusingly named after a long-gone restaurant that was itself named after the Queen's Surf surf break, back to the west off central Waikīkī.

Waikīkī Aquarium

2777 Kalākaua Ave. Daily 9am–5pm; adults $9, seniors and students $6, ages 13–17 $4, ages 5–12 $2; ⓦ www.waikikiaquarium.com. A few minutes' walk east along the Kapiʻolani Park waterfront from Waikīkī Beach stands the disappointingly small Waikīkī Aquarium. Windows in its indoor galleries offer views into the turquoise world of Hawaiian reef fish, among them the lurid red frogfish – an ugly brute that squats splay-footed on the rocks waiting to eat unwary passersby – and a teeming mass of small sharks. The highlight has to be the "leafy sea dragon," a truly bizarre Australian relative of the relatively normal seahorse; there's also a whole tank devoted to sea life from Hanauma Bay (see p.122). Outside, the mocked-up "edge of the reef," complete with artificial tide pools, feels a bit pointless with the real thing just a few feet away. Nearby is a long tank of Hawaiian monk seals, dog-like not only in appearance but also in their willingness to perform tawdry tricks for snacks. As well as a description of traditional fish farming, there's a display of the modern equivalent, in which *mahi mahi* fish grow from transparent eggs to glistening six-footers in what resemble lava lamps.

War Memorial Natatorium

A short way past the Aquarium stands the solemn concrete facade of the decaying War Memorial Natatorium. This curious combination of World War I memorial and swimming pool, with seating for 2500 spectators, was opened with a 100-meter swim by Duke Kahanamoku (see p.49) in 1927. During its inaugural championships, Johnny "Tarzan" Weissmuller set world records in the 100-, 400-, and 800-meter races.

Ironically, the Natatorium never really recovered from being used for training by the US Navy during World War II, and for

▼ MONK SEAL AT WAIKĪKĪ AQUARIUM

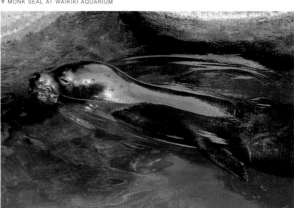

▲ SANS SOUCI BEACH

many years it has remained in a very sorry state indeed, despite constant proposals for its restoration.

Sans Souci Beach

Palm-fringed Sans Souci Beach, just beyond the Natatorium, commemorates one of Waikīkī's earliest guesthouses, built in 1884 and twice stayed in by Robert Louis Stevenson. In addition to being sheltered enough for young children, the beach also offers decent snorkeling. That's unusual for Waikīkī, where most of the reef has been suffocated by dumped sand. The *New Otani Kaimana Beach Hotel* (see p.172), now occupying the site of the *Sans Souci*, marks the return of buildings to the shoreline and is as far as most visitors would think to stroll along Waikīkī Beach. However, beyond it lies the Outrigger Canoe Club Beach, which was leased in 1908 by the club on the condition that its waters be set aside for surfing, canoeing, and ocean sports. The club headquarters was later replaced by the first of the *Outrigger* chain of hotels, but the ocean remains the preserve of surfers and snorkelers.

Kaluahole Beach

As Kalākaua Avenue heads out of Waikīkī beyond the Outrigger Canoe Club Beach, curving away from the shoreline to join Diamond Head Road and skirt the base of the volcano, it passes a little scrap of sandy beach known as Kaluahole Beach or Diamond Head Beach. Though too small for anyone to wants to spend much time on the beach itself, it does offer some quite good swimming, and makes a good launching-point for windsurfers.

Diamond Head Beach Park and beyond

The coast immediately to the east of Kaluahole Beach, officially Diamond Head Beach Park, is much too rocky and exposed for ordinary swimmers. It is, however, noteworthy as the site of the 55-foot Diamond Head Lighthouse, built in 1899 and still in use. The area also has a reputation as a nudist hangout, especially popular with gay men.

A short distance further on, the highway, by now raised well above sea level, rounds the point of Diamond Head; the island of Molokai to the east is visible across the water on clear days. Little scraps of sand cling here and there to the shoreline, but those who pick their way down to the ocean from the three roadside lookouts that constitute Kuilei Cliffs Beach Park tend to be keen surfers.

Opposite the intersection where Diamond Head Road loops back inland and Kahāla Avenue continues beside the ocean, Ka'alāwai Beach, at the end of short Kulumanu Place, is a narrow patch of white sand favored by snorkelers and surfers. It is brought to a halt by Black Point, where lava flowing from Diamond Head into the sea created Oahu's southernmost point.

Diamond Head

The craggy 762-foot pinnacle of Diamond Head, immediately southeast along the coast from Waikīkī, is among the youngest of the chain of volcanic cones that stretch across southeast Oahu. All were created within the last few hundred thousand years by brief, spectacular blasts of the Ko'olau vent. The most recent date back less than ten thousand years, and further eruptions are possible. Diamond Head itself was formed in a few days or even hours.

Ancient Hawaiians knew Diamond Head as either Lei'ahi ("wreath of fire," a reference to beacons lit on the summit to guide canoes) or Lae'ahi ("brow of the yellow-fin tuna"). They built several *heiaus* in and around it, slid down its walls to Waikīkī on *hōlua* land-sleds as sport, and threw convicted criminals from the rim. Its modern name derives from the mistake of a party of English sailors early in the nineteenth century, who stumbled across what they thought were diamonds on its slopes and rushed back to town with glittering but worthless calcite crystals.

For most of the twentieth century, the interior was sealed off by the US armed forces. Only in the 1960s was it reopened as the Diamond Head State Monument public park.

Access to the crater is via a short road tunnel that drills through the surrounding walls from the peak's *mauka* (inland) side. The entrance is around two miles by road from Waikīkī; it's not a particularly pleasant walk, so most people either drive or take the bus. Buses #22 and #58 from Waikīkī climb up Monsarrat Avenue past the zoo

▼ DIAMOND HEAD

▲ DIAMOND HEAD SUMMIT

to join Diamond Head Road, and stop not far from the tunnel; if you're driving, you can also follow the shoreline highway below the mountain and climb the same road from the bottom.

Inside Diamond Head: the climb to the rim

Daily 6am–6pm. $5 per vehicle, or $1 per walk-in hiker. Because the floor of the crater stands well above sea level – it's gradually filling in as the walls erode – Diamond Head is not quite so dramatic from the inside. In fact, the lawns of the crater interior are oddly bland, almost suburban. Often parched, but a vivid green after rain, they're still dotted with little-used military installations.

The main reason visitors come here is to hike the hot half-hour trail up to the rim, for a grand panorama of Oahu's southern coast. So many walkers hit the trail each day, many of them in large organized groups, and not a few undertaking the whole thing as a joyless endurance test, that this is very far from a wilderness experience, and serious hikers looking for great natural splendors are advised to head elsewhere. Not that this is an easy climb; it's surprisingly steep, with

several long concrete staircases, and it's very exposed to the morning sun, so unprepared tourists often end up in considerable distress. Be sure to bring water, and wear suitable footwear and a hat.

Having first climbed slowly away from the crater floor, the paved trail meanders up the inside walls. Many of the holes visible but out of reach on the hillside are ancient burial caves. Before long, you enter the vast network of ugly military bunkers and passageways that riddle the crater. After passing through the first long, dark, and cramped tunnel – watch out for the bolts poking from the ceiling – take time to catch your breath before tackling the very tall, narrow flight of yellow-painted concrete steps that leads up between two high walls to the right.

At the top of the steps, you come to another tunnel, then climb a dark spiral staircase through four or so cramped tiers of fortifications, equipped with eye-slit windows and camouflaged from above. Beyond that, a final outdoor staircase leads to the summit, with its sweeping views of Waikīkī and Honolulu.

Weary hikers who can't face the walk back to Waikīkī can catch the waiting taxis in the parking lot back on the crater floor.

Shops

Bailey's
517 Kapahulu Ave ☎ 808/734-7628, ⓦ alohashirts.com. Daily 10am–6pm. Wonderfully friendly treasure trove of a place – part gallery, part thrift store, part discount outlet – that sells thousands of colorful aloha shirts. Pick up second-hand Sig Zane, Reyn's, and Tori Richard shirts here at good prices ($4–20), as well as authentic 1940s specimens. The finest antique beauties, costing thousands of dollars, are displayed on the wall.

Kahāla Mall
4211 Wai'alae Ave ☎ 808/732-7736, ⓦ www.kahalamallcenter.com. Mon–Sat 10am–9pm, Sun 10am–5pm. Just a couple of miles from Waikīkī, *mauka* of Diamond Head, Kahāla Mall is almost as chic as – though smaller and far less frenzied than – Ala Moana, and tends to attract local rather than international customers. As well as Macy's, Longs Drugs, Banana Republic, an eight-screen movie theater, and an assortment of restaurants, it holds an excellent Barnes & Noble bookstore, along with a branch of Reyn's (see p.94) for aloha wear and a Compleat Kitchen (see p.93) for Hawaiian foodie gifts.

Cafés

Leonard's Bakery
933 Kapahulu Ave ☎ 808/737-5591. Sun–Thurs 6am–9pm, Fri & Sat 6am–10pm. Long-standing Portuguese bakery on the northeastern fringes of Waikīkī, renowned for its delicious, very inexpensive, desserts and the wildly popular sugary and donut-like malassadas.

Restaurants

Diamond Head Grill
W Honolulu, 2885 Kalākaua Ave ☎ 808/922-3734, ⓦ www.w-dhg.com. Daily 7–10.30am & 6–10pm. Over-designed hotel restaurant, kitted out with lots of gleaming metal and specializing in Pacific Rim cuisine. The food is French-influenced-fussy and good, with appetizers like ginger and *ahi* tartar ($13) or foie gras ($19), and entrees such as rack of New Zealand lamb ($40) or roasted *walu* ($34). Despite the name, the only views you get at dinnertime are of the long curving bar. Breakfast is rather more ordinary hotel food.

Hau Tree Lanai
New Otani Kaimana Beach Hotel, 2863 Kalākaua Ave ☎ 808/921-7066. Daily 7–11am, Mon–Sat, 11.30am–2pm & 5.30–9pm, Sun 10am–2pm & 5.30–9pm. Open-air oceanfront restaurant, set beneath the shade of two magnificent spreading *hau* trees beside Sans Souci Beach. Well away from the fray of Waikīkī Beach, it's a peaceful, relaxing spot, perfect for romantic sunsets. Cuisine is mostly continental/American, but with added Pacific Rim touches: choose from top-quality breakfasts (go for the sweetbread French toast with coco-macadamia nut, lunches ranging from sandwiches to crab-cake burgers or seared garlic *ahi* (around $15), or dinner entrees like duck confit or seafood mixed grill ($25–35).

Olive Tree Café

4614 Kīlauea Ave ☎ 808/737-0303.
Daily 5–10pm. Simple, understated
Greek deli, adjoining but not
technically within Kahāla Mall,
with some outdoor seating. The
value is unbeatable, and the food
is great, ranging from refreshing
tomato and feta cheese salads to a
lovely ceviche of New Zealand
mussels ($7), to souvlaki skewers
of chicken or fish ($9–11). No
credit cards.

Sam Choy's Diamond Head

449 Kapahulu Ave ☎ 808/732-8645,
ⓦ www.samchoy.com. Mon–Thurs
5.30–10pm, Fri & Sat 5–11pm, Sun
9.30am–2pm & 5.30–10pm. Usually
buzzing with delighted and
dressed-up locals, this "New
Hawaiian" restaurant – basically
Pacific Rim, with a Hawaiian
emphasis – showcases the cuisine
of TV chef Sam Choy. Though
the location, a mile or so
northeast of Waikīkī, is
unprepossessing, the dining
room itself is comfortable and
relaxed, lined with local art
and with a bustling open
kitchen; the food, of course, is
splendid. The $25–33 entrees,
such as seafood *laulau* (steamed
in *ti* leaves) and *wasabi*-crusted
ono, are deliciously flavored with
local herbs and spices; to start,
don't miss Choy's trademark
fried *poke* ($11). The $25
Sunday brunch buffet includes
poke done five ways, macadamia
nut-crusted chicken and *kālua*
pig.

His other Honolulu restaurant,
Sam Choy's Breakfast, Lunch and
Crab, is reviewed on p.97.

Downtown Honolulu

Although the city as a whole consists of a long, narrow strip sandwiched between the sea and the Koʻolau mountains, downtown Honolulu is compact and easy to explore. The administrative heart of first the kingdom, and now the state, of Hawaii, it is actually located a few blocks west of where the city originated, which is now Chinatown. Today, the downtown focuses on the cluster of buildings that surround ʻIolani Palace, home to Hawaii's last monarchs. This is certainly an attractive district, with several well-preserved historic buildings, and a number of excellent galleries and museums, but it's not a very lively one. At lunchtime on weekdays office workers scurry through the streets, but the rest of the time the contrast with the frenzy of Waikīkī is striking. With few shops, bars, or restaurants to lure outsiders, the whole place is usually empty by 8pm.

ʻIolani Palace

364 S King St. Guided tours Tues–Sat 9–11.15am, every 20min; adults $20, ages 5–12 $5, under-5s not admitted; reservations strongly advised, on ☎808/522-0832, ⓦwww.iolanipalace.org. Audio tours Tues–Sat 11.45am–3pm; adults $12, ages 5–12 $5, under-5s not admitted. Basement galleries Tues–Sat 9am–4.30pm; adults $6, ages 5–12 $3, under-5s admitted free. Stately ʻIolani Palace, dominating downtown from the center of its spacious gardens, was the official home of the last two monarchs of Hawaii. It was built for King David Kalākaua in 1882, near the site of a previous palace that had been destroyed by termites, and

▼ ORCHESTRA PERFORMANCE ON THE ʻIOLANI PALACE LAWN

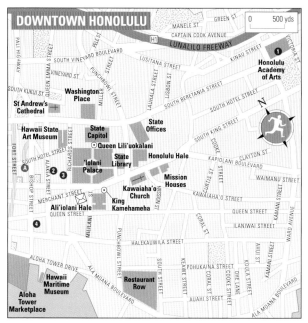

RESTAURANTS AND CAFÉS			ACCOMMODATION	
Café Laniakea	**3**	The Mandalay **2**	ResortQuest at the Executive Center	**A**
Honolulu Café	**4**	Pavilion Café **1**		

he lived here until his death in 1891. For his sister and successor, Queen Lili'uokalani, it was first a palace, and then, after her overthrow in 1893, a prison. It then became the Hawaiian state capitol building, before being turned into a museum on the completion of the new Capitol in 1969.

Visitors can see the palace in three different ways. The state apartments on the first floor, and the royal family's private quarters on the second floor, can be seen on guided tours in the morning only, or on self-guided audio tours later on. The self-guided basement galleries are open to visitors on either kind of tour, or you can also pay to access only those galleries.

Apart from its *koa*-wood floors and staircase, the palace contains little that is distinctively Hawaiian. In the largest of the state rooms downstairs, the Throne Room, Kalākaua held formal balls to celebrate his coronation and fiftieth birthday, and Lili'uokalani was tried for treason. Other reception rooms lead off from the grand central hall, with all available wall space taken up by formal portraits of Hawaiian and other monarchs. Though the plush upstairs bedrooms feel similarly impersonal, there's one touching exhibit – the glass case in the front room contains a quilt made by Queen Lili'uokalani during her eight months under house arrest.

▲ 'IOLANI PALACE

Prize items in the display cases in the basement include two wooden calabashes presented to King Kalākaua on his fiftieth birthday in 1886. One, the tall, slender *ipu* of Lono'ikimakahiki I, was then said to be five hundred years old. Retrieved from the royal burial ground at Ka'awaloa on the Big Island, it was said in legend to have once held all the winds of the world. Among other extraordinary treasures are a feather cloak that Kamehameha I seized from his defeated rival Kīwala'o in 1782 Kalākaua's own crown; and a brooch that Queen Lili'uokalani wore to Queen Victoria's Golden Jubilee celebrations in 1887.

The palace's ticket office is housed in the castellated 'Iolani Barracks on the west side of the grounds, an odd structure that predates the palace by about fifteen years, and also holds a gift store.

Queen Lili'uokalani Statue

On the northern side of 'Iolani Palace, beyond the impressive banyan tree at the foot of the palace steps, a walkway separates the grounds from the State Capitol to the north. At its center, a statue of Queen Lili'uokalani looks haughtily towards the state's present-day legislators. Festooned with *leis* and plumeria blossoms, she's depicted holding copies of her mournful song *Aloha 'Oe*, the Hawaiian creation chant known as the *Kumulipo*, and her draft Constitution of 1893, which precipitated the coup d'état against her.

The State Capitol

415 S Beretania St. Hawaii's State Capitol is a bizarre edifice, propped up on pillars, and with each of its two legislative chambers shaped like a volcano. It took little more than twenty years from its opening in 1969 for flaws in its design to force its closure for extensive and very expensive rebuilding. In front of the main entrance, there's a peculiar cubic statue of Father Damien (see p.52) created by Marisol Escobar in 1968. Well-tended memorials to Hawaiians who died in Korea and Vietnam stand in the grounds to the west.

▲ FATHER DAMIEN STATUE

Washington Place

320 S Beretania St. Free tours available for groups of up to 12, Mon–Fri by appointment; reservations must be made at least 48 hours in advance on ☎808/586-0248. Though Punchbowl Crater (see p.101) looms large as you look north from the Capitol, and you may be able to spot visitors on the rim, it's a long way away by road. Much closer at hand, across Beretania Street, is the white-columned, Colonial-style mansion known as Washington Place. During the 1860s, Queen Lili'uokalani resided here as plain Mrs Dominis, wife to the governor of Hawaii under King Kamehameha V. After her dethronement she returned to live here as a private citizen once more, and died at the mansion in 1917. It became the official residence of the governor of Hawaii five years later, although the present governor actually lives in a separate house in the grounds.

St Andrew's Cathedral

Behind Washington Place, and a short distance to the east, rises the central tower of St Andrew's Cathedral. Work began on this Gothic-influenced Episcopal church in 1867, in realization of plans formed ten years previously by King Kamehameha IV, who wanted to encourage Anglican missionaries to come to Hawaii to counterbalance the prevailing Puritanism of their American counterparts. Construction work only ended in 1958, with the completion of the Great West Window, a stained-glass rendition of the story of Hawaiian Christianity.

The Kamehameha Statue

Downtown's best-known landmark, a flower-bedecked, gilt statue of Kamehameha the Great (1758–1819), stares northwards across King Street towards 'Iolani Palace from outside Ali'iolani Hale. The first man to rule all the islands of Hawaii, Kamehameha is depicted wearing the *'ahu'ula* (royal cloak), *malo* (loincloth), *ka'ei* (sash), and *mahiole* (feather helmet), and clutching a spear. The work of Thomas R. Gould, an American sculptor based in Florence, the statue was commissioned by the Hawaiian legislature in 1878 to celebrate the centenary of the arrival of Captain Cook. On its way to Hawaii, however, it was lost in a shipwreck, so a second copy was cast and dispatched. That arrived in 1880 and was unveiled by

▼ KAMEHAMEHA STATUE

King Kalākaua at his coronation in 1883; surplus insurance money from the lost statue paid for the sequence of four panels depicting scenes from Kamehameha's life around its base. Meanwhile, the original statue, which was found floating off the Falkland Islands, was purchased by a whaling captain in Port Stanley, and also turned up in Hawaii. It was packed off to Kamehameha's birthplace on the Big Island. Ceremonies are held at the Honolulu statue on June 11 each year to mark Kamehameha Day, a state holiday.

Aliʻiolani Hale

417 S King St. Mon–Fri 9am–4pm; free; ⊛ www.judiciaryhistorycenter.org. Erected in 1874, the stately Aliʻiolani Hale – "House of the Heavenly King" in Hawaiian – was Hawaii's first library and national museum; it was also the first building taken over by the conspirators who overthrew the monarchy in 1893. Throughout its history, however, its main function has been as the home of the state's Supreme Court. The first floor houses the fascinating Judiciary History Center. This outlines the story of Hawaiian law from the days of the ancient

kapu onwards and chronicles the Supreme Court's role in replacing the tradition of collective land ownership with the concept of private ownership. There's also a scale model of Honolulu in 1850, watched over by the now-vanished fort and with thatched huts still dotted among its Victorian mansions.

Hawaii State Art Museum

250 S Hotel St. Tues–Sat 10am–4pm; free; ☎ 808/586-0900, ⊛ www.hawaii .gov/sfca. Immediately west of ʻIolani Palace, across Richards Street from the palace ticket office but entered via South Hotel Street, the excellent Hawaii State Art Museum fills the second floor of an impressive 1920s Spanish Mission building with displays of the state's collection of contemporary art. Broadly speaking, the ʻEwa galleries to the west hold small-scale works in different media that explore Hawaii's natural and urban environment, including Mark Hamasaki's hard-hitting photos of the devastation caused by the H-3 freeway project. Look out too for the most popular painting, taken from Masami Teraoka's hilarious Hanauma Bay Series, in which local snorkelers are deliberately styled after Japan's *ukiyo-e* tradition of brightly colored woodblock prints. Under the title "Precious Resources: The Land and the Sea", the Diamond Head galleries to the east feature displays on Pacific voyaging, including a model of the Hōkūleʻa canoe, some fine *koa*-wood carved bowls, and large, lyrical paintings of Hawaiian landscapes.

▼ HAWAII STATE ART MUSEUM

▲ THE STATE SEAL OF HAWAII

Kawaiahaʻo Church

957 Punchbowl St. Mon–Fri 8am–4pm.
Although Kawaiahaʻo Church,
just east of ʻIolani Palace near the
junction of Punchbowl and King
streets, was erected in 1842, less
than twenty years after the first
Christian missionaries came to
Hawaii, it was the fifth church to
stand on this site. According to
its Protestant minister, Rev
Hiram Bingham, each of the four
predecessors was a thatched "cage
in a haymow." This one, by
contrast, was built with
thousand-pound chunks of living
coral, hacked from the reef. It's
not especially huge, but the
columned portico is grand
enough, topped by a foursquare
clock-tower.

Inside, broad balconies run
down both sides of the nave,
lined with royal portraits. Below,
plaques on the walls honor early
figures of Hawaiian Christianity,
such as Henry ʻOpukahaʻia. The
plushest pews – at the back of the
church, upholstered in velvet and
marked off by *kahili* standards –
were reserved for royalty.

The small mausoleum in the
grounds fronting the church
holds the remains of King
Lunalilo, who
ruled for less
than two years
after his election
in 1872. Feeling
slighted that his
mother's body
had not been
removed from
the churchyard
to the royal
mausoleum (see
p.109), he chose
to be buried here
instead. The rest
of the graves in
the cemetery
around the back
serve as a brief
introduction to Hawaii's
nineteenth-century missionary
elite, with an abundance of
Castles and Cookes, Alexanders
and Baldwins, and the only
president of the Republic,
Sanford B. Dole.

The Mission Houses

553 S King St. Mission Houses tours
Tues, Wed, Fri & Sat 11am & 2.45pm,
Thurs 2pm; adults $10, under-19s $6;
☎808/531-0481, ⓦwww
.missionhouses.org. Visitor center
Tues–Sat 10am–4pm; $5, or $13
combination with tour. The lives of
Hawaii's first Christian
missionaries are recalled in the
restored Mission Houses behind
Kawaiahaʻo Church. Standing
cheek by jowl along King Street,
these three nineteenth-century
buildings commemorate the
pioneers of the Sandwich Islands
Mission, who arrived from
Boston in 1820. The only way to
see inside the actual buildings is
on a guided tour, but displays in
the separate visitor center provide
a sense of the missionary impact
from a native Hawaiian
perspective, and include models
of the mission station as it stood
in the 1820s and 1850s.

The oldest edifice, the two-story Frame House, was shipped in whole from New England in 1821. Reluctant to let outsiders build permanent structures, the king only allowed it to go up with the words "when you go away, take everything with you." Local fears that its cellar held weapons for a planned takeover of the islands were allayed when Kamehameha's principal advisor, Kalanimoku, built a house with a larger cellar across the street. The house, whose tiny windows were entirely unsuited to the heat of Honolulu, was home to four missionary families. A kitchen had to be added because cooking outdoors attracted too much attention from the islanders, as it was *kapu* for women to prepare food.

One of the missionaries' first acts, in 1823, was to set up the Print House, which produced the first Hawaiian-language Bible – *Ka Palapala Hemolele*. The current building – not the original, but its 1841 replacement – holds a replica of its imported Ramage printing press, whose limitations were among the reasons why to this day the Hawaiian alphabet only has twelve letters.

The largest of the three buildings, the Chamberlain House, started life in 1831 as the mission storehouse. As the missionary families became increasingly embroiled in the economy of the islands, that role turned it into the commercial headquarters of Castle and Cooke, one of the original "Big Five".

Honolulu Academy of Arts

900 S Beretania St. Tues–Sat 10am–4.30pm, Sun 1–5pm; tours Tues–Sat 10.15am, 11.30am & 1.30pm, Sun 1.15pm; open 11am–5pm, with free admission on third Sun of month; otherwise $7, seniors and students $4, under-13s free; ☎808/532-8700, ⓦwww.honoluluacademy.org. Honolulu residents take great pride in the stunning fine art at the Academy of Arts. Few tourists find their way to this elegant, Eastern-influenced former private home, half a mile east of the Capitol and centered around open courtyards and fountains, but two or three hours wandering the galleries is time well spent.

The bulk of the Academy's superb collection of paintings are housed around the Mediterranean Court, to the right of the entrance. Highlights include Van Gogh's *Wheat Field*, Gauguin's *Two Nudes on a Tahitian Beach*, and one of Monet's *Water Lilies*. Under the theme of "East meets West," the final parts of this section explore cross-cultural contacts between Europe, India, and China. An entire room on Captain Cook and the Pacific is papered with gloriously romantic French wallpaper from around 1804.

An even larger area on the first floor is devoted to Asian art and artifacts, displaying Korean, Japanese, "pan-Asian Buddhist," and, especially, Chinese works. Among the latter are beautiful Neolithic-era ceramics, four-thousand-year-old jade blades, and columns from a two-thousand-year-old Han tomb. There then follows a cornucopia of masterpieces: Buddhist and Shinto deities, plus *netsuke* (toggles) and samurai armor from Japan; Tibetan *thangkas* (religious images); Indian carvings ranging from Rajasthani sandstone screens to a stone Chola statue of Krishna; Mayan effigies; Melanesian masks; and pottery from the pueblos of Arizona and New Mexico.

▲ HONOLULU ACADEMY OF ARTS

One last street-level gallery holds the Academy's Modern and Contemporary collection, which ranges from a Francis Bacon triptych to a Nam June Paik video installation.

Upstairs on the second floor of the newer Luce Pavilion, most of the works in The Arts of Hawaii are of mainly historic interest. Nonetheless, the early depictions of Hawaii here by Western artists are well worth seeing. These include an 1816 painting of Kailua on the Big Island by the Russian Louis Choris – whose well-known portrait *Kamehameha in Red Vest* is here only as a reproduction – and several dramatic renditions of the changing face of the volcano at Kīlauea. A few key works by Georgia O'Keeffe, who was enamored of the islands' verdant cliffs and waterfalls, demonstrate her distinctively surreal, sexually charged style.

Shops

The Academy Shop

Honolulu Academy of Arts, 900 S Beretania St ☎808/532-8703 or 3688, ⓦwww.honoluluacademy.org. Tues–Sat 10am–4.30pm, Sun 1–5pm. A very good little museum store, whose books, notebooks, and journals, prints, posters, postcards, and jewelry all reflect the broad scope of the collection, with some especially good stuff from the Pacific Islands and the Far East.

Cafés

Honolulu Café

741 Bishop St ☎808/533-1555. Mon–Fri 6am–5pm. Busy, large downtown coffee bar, at the south end of Bishop Street, with seating indoors and outside. Open weekdays only, it serves espressos and smoothies plus

gourmet salads and sandwiches
for $7–10, and daily specials.

Restaurants

Café Laniakea
YWCA, 1040 Richards St ☎808/524-
8789. Mon–Fri 11am–2pm. Lunch-
only downtown cafeteria, very
close to 'Iolani Palace, promising
"local first, organic whenever
possible, with Aloha always". Lots
of inexpensive vegetarian dishes,
with salads at $8–10, along with
sandwiches ($9–10) and daily
specials such as a half chicken or
grilled salmon ($11–13).

The Mandalay
1055 Alakea St ☎808/525-8585.
Daily 10.30am–10pm. Smart,
modern but not hugely
atmospheric Chinese restaurant

in the heart of the downtown
business district. What really
pulls in the lunchtime office
crowd is the made-to-order dim
sum (served 10.30am–5pm),
which you choose from an
illustrated sheet rather than a
passing cart, though the
classic Cantonese entrees
(typically $15–25) are good
enough to merit above-average
prices.

Pavilion Café
Honolulu Academy of Arts, 900
S Beretania St ☎808/532-8734.
Tues–Sat 11.30am–2pm, plus 3rd
Sun of each month 11.30am–2pm.
With its zestful Mediterranean
sandwiches and salads, this
appealing little lunch-only
courtyard bistro makes the
perfect midday stop for anyone
exploring downtown.

Chinatown

Barely five minutes' walk west of 'Iolani Palace, a pair of matching stone dragons flank either side of Hotel Street, marking the transition between downtown Honolulu and the oldest part of the city, Chinatown. For well over a century, this was renowned as the city's red-light district. Though almost all the pool halls, massage parlors, and tawdry bars that formerly lined the narrow streets have now gone, and indeed the area is currently booming, its fading green clapboard storefronts and bustling market ambience still make Chinatown seem like another world. As it changes, futuristic elements blend with the relics of the past to create a hybrid of old and new, East and West. Cosmopolitan, atmospheric, and historic in equal proportions, it's the one local neighborhood that's genuinely fun to explore on your own.

While Chinatown certainly retains its traditional Asian flavor, it's also attracted a considerable influx in recent years of hip, creative types, who are most evident in its lively art scene. The regular First Friday event, in which galleries stay open 5–8pm on the first Friday of each month, enabling visitors to take early-evening strolls from gallery to gallery, has been so successful that it has recently spawned the self-explanatory Second Saturday and Third Thursday programs.

Of the district's two main axes, N Hotel and Maunakea streets, Hotel Street best lives up to the old lowlife reputation, with neon signs advertising long-gone fleshpots – *Club Hubba Hubba Topless-Bottomless* to name but one – and drunken sailors lurching to and from assorted

▼ CHINATOWN APOTHECARY

sawdust-floored bars. At the intersection with Maunakea Street stands the ornate hundred-year-old facade of Wo Fat's *Chop Sui* restaurant, now occupied by a Chinese supermarket.

Many of Chinatown's old walled courtyards have been converted into open malls, but the businesses within remain much the same. Apothecaries and herbalists weigh out dried leaves in front of endless arrays of

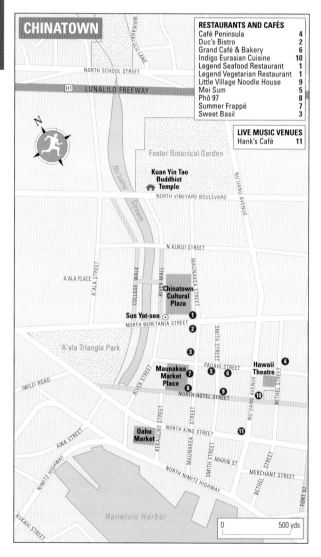

CHINATOWN

RESTAURANTS AND CAFÉS
Café Peninsula	4
Duc's Bistro	2
Grand Café & Bakery	6
Indigo Eurasian Cuisine	10
Legend Seafood Restaurant	1
Legend Vegetarian Restaurant	1
Little Village Noodle House	9
Mei Sum	5
Phỏ 97	8
Summer Frappé	7
Sweet Basil	3

LIVE MUSIC VENUES
Hank's Café	11

WAIKAHALULU LANE

NORTH SCHOOL STREET

H1 LUNALILO FREEWAY

N

Foster Botanical Garden

Nuʻuanu Stream

Kuan Yin Tao Buddhist Temple

NORTH VINEYARD BOULEVARD

NUʻUANU AVENUE

N KUKUI STREET

Aʻala PLACE

Aʻala STREET

COLLEGE WALK

RIVER MALL

MAUNAKEA STREET

Chinatown Cultural Plaza

Sun Yat-sen

NORTH BERETANIA STREET

SMITH STREET

Aʻala Triangle Park

RIVER STREET

PAUAHI STREET

Maunakea Market Place

Hawaiʻi Theatre

BETHEL STREET

IWILEI ROAD

NORTH HOTEL STREET

NUʻUANU AVENUE

KEKAULIKE STREET

NORTH KING STREET

MAUNAKEA STREET

SMITH STREET

Oahu Market

MARIN ST

NIMITZ HIGHWAY

AWA STREET

NORTH NIMITZ HIGHWAY

BETHEL STREET

MERCHANT STREET

FORT ST

KUKAHI STREET

Honolulu Harbor

0   500 yds

bottles, shelves, and wooden cabinets, while groups of deft-fingered women gather around tables to thread *leis*. Every hole-in-the-wall store holds a fridge bursting with colorful blooms, and appetizing food smells waft from backstreet bakeries.

Hawaii Theatre

1130 Bethel St. Tours Tues 11am, $5. Performance schedules and tickets ☎808/528-0506 or ⓦwww .hawaiitheatre.com. The leading local landmark in Chinatown is the painstakingly restored Art Deco Hawaii Theatre, on Bethel Street near the border with downtown. Guided tours take place every Tuesday, at 11am, but a far better way to appreciate the gorgeous interior is by attending one of its varied programs or (mostly one-off or short-run) performances.

Oahu Market and Maunakea Marketplace

It's easy to while away an enjoyable hour or two in Chinatown exploring the many pleasures of its food markets. Perhaps the finest of these, bursting with Oriental food specialties and busy every morning with bargain-seeking locals, is the Oahu Market, on N King and Kekaulike. One of the fastest-selling items is *ahi* (yellow-fin tuna), used for making *sashimi* or *poke*, but this is also the place to go if you're looking for pig snouts or salmon heads.

For the best selection of ready-to-eat food, visit the Maunakea Marketplace, a couple of blocks north and entered from either

▲ OAHU MARKET

PLACES Chinatown

Hotel or Maunakea streets. Another tempting food market, piled high with shiny eggplants, great mountains of gnarled ginger roots, and twitchy live crabs, it also has a good little food court, inside the main building. The temperature is likely to be sweltering, but the choice of cuisines – Filipino, Vietnamese, Korean, Thai, Malaysian, Hong Kong – is good, and at the lowest prices in Honolulu.

Nu'uanu Stream

Chinatown is bordered to the west by Nu'uanu Stream, which flows down to Honolulu Harbor. River Street, running alongside, becomes a restaurant-filled pedestrian mall between Beretania and Kukui streets. At the port end stands a *lei*-swaddled statue of Sun Yat-sen, while over Kukui Street at the opposite end is the tiny, ornate-roofed Lum Hai So Tong Taoist temple, erected by a "friendly society" in 1899 and now perched above a couple of little stores. Most of the interior of the block next to the mall is occupied by the Chinatown Cultural Plaza, filled with slightly tacky souvenir stores

If you'd like to join an organized **walking tour of Chinatown**, contact the Hawaii Heritage Center, 1168 Smith St (Tues & Fri 9.30am; $10; ☎808/521-2749) or the Chinatown Museum (min group of 4; Mon–Sat 10.30am; $10; ☎808/595-3358).

▲ THREADING A LEI

and conventional businesses that cater to the Chinese community.

Foster Botanical Garden

50 N Vineyard Boulevard. Daily 9am–4.30pm, last admission 4pm; adults $5, under-13s $1; guided tours, no extra charge, Mon–Sat 1pm. At the top end of River Street, and entered via a short driveway that leads off N Vineyard Boulevard beside the Kuan Yin Buddhist temple, is the fourteen-acre Foster Botanical Garden. Established in the mid-nineteenth

The Chinese in Hawaii

At the end of the eighteenth century, within ten years of Captain Cook's arrival in Hawaii, Chinese seamen were jumping ship to seek their fortunes in the land they knew as Tan Hueng Shan, the Sandalwood Mountains. Trading vessels regularly crossed the Pacific between China and Hawaii, and Cantonese merchants and entrepreneurs became a familiar sight in Honolulu. Even the granite that paved the streets of what became Chinatown was brought over from China as ballast in ships.

At first, the majority worked in the sugar plantations of Kauai, but in time the **Chinese** settled increasingly in Honolulu, where "friendly societies" would help new arrivals find their feet. Inevitably, many of these were renegades and outlaws, ranging from gang members to political dissidents. Sun Yat-sen, for example, who became the first President of the Republic of China when the Manchu Dynasty was overthrown in 1911, was educated at 'Iolani School.

By the 1860s there were more Chinese than white residents in Hawaii. With the native Hawaiian population shrinking, the pro-American establishment in Honolulu felt threatened. In response, they maneuvered to ensure that white residents could vote for the national legislature while Asians could not. They also induced the plantations to switch their recruiting policies and focus on other parts of the globe.

By the close of the nineteenth century, **Chinatown** was at its zenith. Its crowded lanes held more than seven thousand people, including Japanese and Hawaiians as well as Chinese. When bubonic plague was detected in December 1899, however, city authorities decided to prevent its spread by systematic burning. The first few controlled burns were effective, but on January 20, 1900, a small fire started at Beretania and Nu'uanu rapidly turned into a major conflagration. The flames destroyed Kaumakapili Church as well as a 38-acre swathe that reached to within a few yards of the waterfront. White-owned newspapers were soon rhapsodizing about the opportunity to expand downtown Honolulu, convincing the Chinese community, which never received adequate compensation, that the destruction was at the very least welcome and at worst deliberate. Nonetheless, Chinatown was rebuilt, and the fact that almost all its surviving structures date from that rebuilding gives it an appealing architectural harmony.

▲ LUM SAI HO TONG TEMPLE NEAR THE FOSTER BOTANICAL GARDEN

century as a sanctuary for Hawaiian plants and a testing ground for foreign species, it has become one of Honolulu's best-loved city parks. Thanks to the H-1 freeway racing along its northern flank, it's not exactly the quietest of places, but it's usually filled with birds nonetheless. Different sections cover spices and herbs, flowering orchids, and tropical trees from around the world. As well as sausage trees from Mozambique, the latter collection includes a spectacular "cannonball tree", a giant *quipo*, and a *bo* (or *peepal*) tree supposedly descended from the *bo* tree at Bodh Gaya in north India where the Buddha achieved enlightenment.

Shops

AmeriComb House
1428 Liliha St ☏808/548-2662, ⓦwww.AmeriCombs.com. Daily 10am–6pm. Handmade wooden combs, mirrors, and compacts in a variety of designs, in a shop that proclaims "Beauty always start from the combing".

Bad Sushi
935 River St ☏808/548-7874, ⓦwww.badsushihawaii.com. Daily noon–8pm. Chinatown gets edgy in this fashion boutique, with its hip range of vaguely saucy clothes, beachwear, and funky kung fu fashion.

Chinatown Boardroom
1160 Nu'uanu Ave ☏808/585-7200, ⓦwww.chinatownboardroom.com. Mon, Fri & Sat 11am–6pm; Tues & Thurs 3–6 pm. Another of Chinatown's rash of hip new stores, a surf shop-cum-art gallery, displaying customized boards and local paintings alongside funky flip-flops and shorts.

Xin Xin's Fashion
1011C Maunakea St ☏808/531-8885. Mon–Sat 9.30am–5pm, Sun 9.30am–3pm. One of the better stores for Chinese and Hong Kong fashions, with a good selection of satin cheong sams, pretty parasols, and unusual gifts. The exquisite little paper ornaments, involving such miniature masterpieces as bobbing kimono-clad ladies and

fluttering birds on strings, are a bargain, and easy to carry home.

Cafés

Café Peninsula

1147 Bethel St ☎808/566-6979. Mon–Fri 9am–5pm. Friendly and appealingly eccentric Chinatown coffee shop, on a small coffee-bar row near the Hawaii Theater. Overstuffed with sprawling rattan armchairs and 1970s sofas, offering a quirky selection of books to read and a Chinese pop music soundtrack, it attracts a quiet local crowd of students and business people. Simple plate lunches such as spam with rice and egg ($5), and *saimin* ($4.25), are served, along with sandwiches, bagels, espresso drinks, and iced herbal teas.

Summer Frappé

1120 Maunakea St, store 192 ☎808/722-9291. Daily 7.30am–6pm. Hole-in-the-wall juice and snack bar in the courtyard behind the Maunakea Marketplace food hall. With shaded outdoor seating, it's the perfect place to restore yourself with a delicious fresh smoothie, made with exotic fruits, or a fruity bubble tea studded with tapioca pearls.

Restaurants

Duc's Bistro

1188 Maunakea St ☎808/531-6325. Mon–Sat 11.30am–2pm & 5–10pm. Sophisticated Asian-influenced French restaurant in Chinatown, which hosts live jazz nightly except Thurs. Dinner appetizers ($8–12) include gravadlax, escargots, and, unusually in Hawaii, oysters on the half shell; a basic lemongrass chicken entree costs $14, fancier options like

duck breast in Grand Marnier or flambéed steak are $22–30. Portions and prices are significantly smaller at lunchtime.

Grand Café & Bakery

31 N Pauahi St ☎808/531-0001. Tues–Fri 7am–1.30pm, Sat & Sun 8am–1pm, 1st Fri of month also 5.15–7.45pm. Airy Chinatown restaurant, established in the 1920s, where the appealingly old-fashioned feel extends to the menu. Choose from comfort food – pot roast, meat loaf – or more modern choices like grilled asparagus and poached egg salad and tasty pastries and desserts. Breakfasts are particularly fine, based on tempting dishes like Banana Foster French toast.

Indigo Eurasian Cuisine

1121 Nu'uanu Ave ☎808/521-2900, ⊛www.indigo-hawaii.com. Tues–Thurs 11.30am–2pm & 6–9.30pm, Fri 11.30am–2pm & 6–10pm, Sat 6–10pm. Chinatown's classiest option, a lovely space with indoor and outdoor seating, serves delicious nouvelle "Eurasian" crossover food. In addition to the good value $17 lunch buffet, which includes

▼ INDIGO EURASIAN CUISINE

three types of dim sum, including taro dumplings and goat cheese wontons, you can select from a broad range of dim sum ($7–12), including "thousand loved crab cakes", and entrees like wokked "Buddhist" vegetables ($16). Dinner entrees (around $19–30) include Shanghai duck with soft bao buns, ginger ham shanks, and moi roasted in a banana leaf. The adjoining late-night *Green Room Lounge* has live music and dancing Tues–Sat.

Legend Seafood Restaurant

100 N Beretania St ☎808/532-1868. Mon–Fri 10.30am–2pm & 5.30–9pm, Sat & Sun 8am–2pm & 5.30–9pm. Chinatown seafood specialist in a modern building whose big plate-glass windows look out over the Nu'uanu Stream. The lunchtime dim sum trolleys are piled with individual portions at $3–5; full Chinese meals, with entrees including whole lobster or crab at $10–20, are served at both lunch and dinner.

Legend Vegetarian Restaurant

100 N Beretania St ☎808/532-8218. Daily except Wed 10.30am–2pm. Bright Chinese vegetarian restaurant in the heart of Chinatown, looking out across the Nu'uanu Stream and open for lunch only. The menu features faux beef balls, cuttlefish, pork ribs, and tenderloin – all the dishes are actually tofu or other organic, vegetarian ingredients shaped and flavored to resemble the specified meats and fishes. There's also a wide selection of vegetarian dim sum, plus conventional vegetable dishes. Entrees are priced well under $10; set meals for four or more work out at around $10 per person. No alcohol is served.

Little Village Noodle House

1113 Smith St ☎808/545-3008. Sun–Thurs 10.30am–10.30pm, Fri & Sat 10.30am–midnight. Smart but friendly restaurant in the heart of Chinatown, offering a perfectly prepared range of delicious Chinese dishes from Singapore noodles ($7.95) through salt and pepper pork ($9.50) to clams in black bean sauce ($13.50). The special Hong Kong menu has congees and noodle soups from $5.

Mei Sum

65 N Pauahi St at Smith ☎808/531-3268. Daily 7am–8.45pm. No-frills, high-quality traditional dim sum restaurant, where the trolleys are heaving all day long with a wide assortment of tasty snacks priced between $2 and $3.15 each. Tasty options include seafood or mushroom chicken dumplings, turnip cake, deep fried scallops in taro leaves, and *char siu* buns. Noodle, rice, and wonton entrees, featuring chicken, prawns, scallops, or calamari, are also available for $7–10 per plate. A full dinner for four is just $36.

Phô 97

176 Maunakea Marketplace, Maunakea St ☎808/538-0708. Mon–Sat 8am–9pm, Sun 8am–7pm. This large Chinatown restaurant, technically in the Maunakea Marketplace but entered direct from Maunakea Street, is the best place to sample Vietnamese *phô* (noodle soup). There are also lots of Cambodian, Thai, and Vietnamese noodle and rice dishes, as well as barbecued pork, simmered catfish, and crab meat soup. The potions are huge, and almost nothing costs more than $7.

Sweet Basil

1152A Maunakea St ☎808/545-5800.

▲ HANK'S CAFÉ

Mon–Thurs 10.30am–2pm, Fri & Sat 10.30am–2pm & 5–9pm. Small and simple, spotless and smart, this lovely Thai restaurant – a rarity in Chinatown – is an absolute winner for its authentic, tasty, and healthy home cooking (with no MSG). The astonishingly good-value lunch buffet ($8.95) includes four hot curries, with a different special every day, plus four zingy fresh Thai salads, two soups and fruit for dessert. A la carte options ($5–15) include simple curries and veggie choices through noodle dishes to sizzling seafood entrees.

Bars

Hank's Café

1038 Nuuanu St, Honolulu ☎ 808/526-1410, ⓦ www.hankscafehonolulu.com. Mon 3–10pm, Tues–Sun 3pm–2am. Small art gallery-cum-bar in Chinatown, with an appealing retro feel, staging regular live music jams, some Hawaiian, some not. On the second floor, in what was once a tattoo parlor – hence the impressive mural – you'll find *The Dragon Upstairs*, which puts on live jazz Thurs–Sun.

Waterfront Honolulu

It's all too easy to forget that central Honolulu stands just a few yards up from the turquoise waters of the Pacific, clean enough here to support conspicuous populations of bright tropical fish. Sadly, pedestrians exploring Chinatown or downtown have to brave the fearsome traffic of the Nimitz Highway in order to reach the ocean. That effort is rewarded by a short but enjoyable stroll along the segment of the waterfront that stretches for a couple of hundred yards east of the venerable Aloha Tower. Until 1857, this area was covered by the waves; then, the city fort, which had previously stood at Fort and Queen streets, was torn down, and the rubble used to fill in a fifteen-acre expanse of the sea floor. Now, in addition to watching the comings and goings of Honolulu Harbor, you can join a sunset dinner cruise or similar expedition from the piers nearby or learn something of the port's history in the Hawaii Maritime Center.

Aloha Tower

Pier 9, Honolulu Harbor. Tower Observation Deck daily 9am–5pm, free; Marketplace stores Mon–Sat 9am–9pm, Sun 9am–6pm; ⓦwww .alohatower.com. The Aloha Tower was built in 1926, as both a control center for the port's traffic and a landmark for arriving cruise passengers. At 184ft high, it was then the tallest building in Honolulu; with its four giant clock-faces, each surmounted by the word "ALOHA," it was also the most photographed. Seventy years of skyscraper construction made it seem progressively smaller and smaller, but the tower returned to prominence a decade ago as the centerpiece of the Aloha Tower Marketplace shopping mall.

With far fewer parking spaces available here than at the major malls, the stores at Aloha Tower are heavily dependent on day-trippers from Waikīkī. After-work downtowners keep the mall's restaurants and music venues busy in the evenings, especially at weekends, but during the day it can seem somewhat forlorn. However, with the mall walkways ending right at the dockside, and several of the restaurants and bars offering large open-air terraces, it still makes an appealing place to get a sense of the ongoing life of the port. Cargo vessels from all over the world tie up alongside, and there's always something going on out in the water.

Taking a free trip up to the tenth-floor Observation Deck of the now rather shabby Aloha Tower itself is also worthwhile. Balconies on each of its four sides, originally used as lookouts by harbor pilots, offer views that are just short of ugly – freeways, airport runways, and grimy

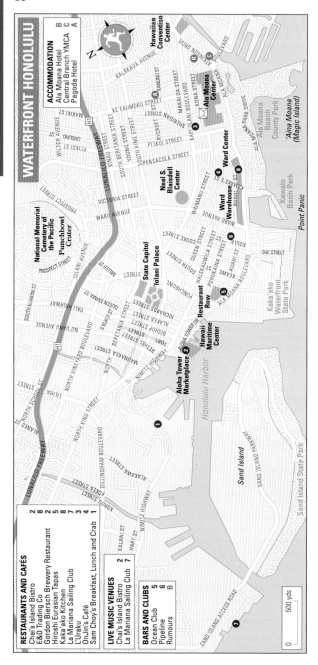

WATERFRONT HONOLULU

▲ EXHIBIT AT THE HAWAII MARITIME CENTER

harbor installations – but provide an excellent orientation to the city. As you look towards Diamond Head, which may well be obscured by haze, the twin pink-trimmed "stereo speakers" of the Waterfront Towers condominiums loom above the black glass of Restaurant Row; meanwhile, Pearl Harbor sprawls to the west, and the green mountains soar inland.

Hawaii Maritime Center

Pier 7, Honolulu Harbor. Daily 8.30am–5pm; adults $7.50, under-18s $4.50; ☎808/536-6373, ⓦwww .bishopmuseum.org. A short walk east of the Aloha Marketplace, the Hawaii Maritime Center illustrates Hawaii's seafaring past in riveting detail. Displays start on the second floor with the voyages of Captain Cook and follow a chronological order. The next section delves into the whaling industry with exhibits such as a huge iron try-pot, and scrimshaw carved by

nineteenth-century seamen on ivory smoothed with sharkskin "sandpaper." The rest of the floor is given over to the growth of tourism and the heyday of cruise ships. Having examined photos of Honolulu Harbor, you can see the whole thing yourself by climbing the 81 steps up an observation tower.

Downstairs, the focus turns to the Polynesian seafaring. A full-sized, double-hulled canoe shows the equipment and cargo carried by the first voyagers. There's also a section on Polynesian tattoos and ancient medicines, along

▼ FALLS OF CLYDE

with photos of Waikīkī's first surfing clubs.

For many visitors, however, the chief attractions are the two vessels moored alongside museum. *The Falls of Clyde* is the only four-masted, full-rigged sailing ship left in the world. Built of wrought iron in Glasgow in 1876, it's also the world's only sail-powered oil tanker; after years of ferrying sugar between California and Hawaii, it was converted to carry petroleum in 1907. Visiting this only partially restored ship today is an eerie experience – its musty old captain's quarters, rusting storage trunks, and discarded ephemera giving it a ghostly feel.

When it's not sailing to Tahiti, New Zealand, or the far reaches of the South Pacific, the replica Polynesian canoe *Hōkūle'a* is moored at the end of the pier. Its voyages have inspired a huge revival of interest in traditional methods of navigation, and parties of eager schoolchildren flock here for close-up inspections. You can only go on board on a guided tour, which normally take place on weekdays only.

The western waterfront: Sand Island

Honolulu Harbor, which is inaccessible to casual viewing west of the Aloha Tower, is a relatively narrow deep-water channel shielded from the open ocean by the bulk of Sand Island. The seaward side of Sand Island is a state park, where the plentiful supply of restrooms, showers, and pavilions does little to alleviate the impression that you're surrounded by an industrial wasteland. There's a certain amount of sandy beach, and locals come to hang out and fish, but it's hard to see why any tourist would drive five miles to

get here. If you insist on doing so, follow Nimitz Highway almost as far as the airport, and then loop back along Sand Island Access Road.

East to Waikīkī: Ala Moana

East of Aloha Tower and the Maritime Center, Ala Moana Boulevard runs along the shoreline towards Waikīkī, passing along the way a few more of Honolulu's main shopping malls – the Ward Warehouse, the Ward Centre, and the pick of the bunch, the Ala Moana Center. Year after year, the stores here seem to increase both in quality and quantity, and for an ever-greater proportion of visitors to Waikīkī, the Ala Moana district is their only foray into Honolulu proper.

Kaka'ako Waterfront Park

The first spot where you can enter the ocean on the way along Ala Moana Boulevard towards Waikīkī is Point Panic in Kaka'ako Waterfront Park. Serious board- and body-surfers swear by its powerful waves, but a lack of sand, an abundance of sharks, and the fact that the surf hammers straight into a stone wall combine to ensure that few visitors are tempted to join them. Even though there's no beach, the park itself is nice enough, with its grassy hills, paved pathways, and pavilions.

Kewalo Basin Park

Kewalo Basin Park, across from the Ward Warehouse, occupies the thin oceanfront groin that shelters the Kewalo Basin harbor, used by several small-boat operators. Though the setting is attractive enough, the park's role as a hangout for local transients makes it a bit of a no-go area for outsiders.

▲ MAGIC ISLAND

Ala Moana Beach County Park

Though tourists tend not to realize it, the long green lawns across Ala Moana Boulevard from the malls flank a superb beach – the long white-sand strand preserved as the Ala Moana Beach County Park. This is where Honolulu city-dwellers come to enjoy excellent facilities and, especially during working hours, a relative absence of crowds. Like most of the beaches in Waikīkī, it's artificial, having been constructed during the 1930s on the site of a garbage dump. Inshore swimming is generally safe and good, and there's some potential for snorkeling around the reef; just watch out for the steep drop-off, only a few yards out at low tide.

'Aina Moana (Magic Island)

At its eastern end, Ala Moana Beach curves out and around a long promontory. Known as Magic Island or 'Aina Moana, this too is artificial. It was one of the most ambitious elements of the state's plans to expand tourism in the early 1960s, the idea being to reclaim an "island" of shallow coral reef, connect it to the mainland, and build luxury hotels on it. The hotels never materialized, so the vast sums of money involved have instead resulted in the creation of a tranquil park with roomy lawns, a gently sloping beach, and a lovely little crescent lagoon at its tip. It's worth wearing reef shoes if you go in the water, however, as the seafloor is rocky.

Malls

Ala Moana Center

1450 Ala Moana Blvd ☎ 808/955-9517, ⒲ www.alamoana.com. Mall: Mon–Thurs 9.30am–9pm, Fri 9.30am–10pm, Sat 8am–10pm, Sun 10am–7pm (store hours vary). In addition to TheBus, daily shuttle buses run to and from Waikīkī; look for the pink trolleys ($2; every 8min Mon–Sat 10am–9.28pm, Sun 10am–7.52pm. A mile west of Waikīkī, Ala Moana has since 1959 been Hawaii's main shopping destination; neighbor-island residents fly to Honolulu specifically in order to shop here. One of the largest open-air malls in the world, currently numbering 260 outlets and growing year on year, it holds several major department stores, including Sears, Macy's, and Neiman Marcus, with couture designers represented by the likes of Armani, Chanel, Burberry, Gucci, Vuitton, and Jimmy Choo, and upscale street-style at Betsey Johnson, DKNY, Diesel, and Shanghai Tang. In

▼ ALA MOANA CENTER

addition to the distinctive stores reviewed below, Hawaii-specific outlets include Tori Richard (see p.54), Cinnamon Girl (see p.53), and Martin and Macarthur (p.54).

Aloha Tower Marketplace

1 Aloha Tower Drive ☎ 808/566-2337, ⓦ www.alohatower.com. Mon–Sat 9am–9pm, Sun 9am–6pm. A little tired, and verging on the downmarket, this breezy outdoor mall has failed to lure significant numbers of tourists away from Ala Moana, but the dockside setting makes it a fun place to wander around. Most of the seventy or so stores are one-of-a-kind rather than chain outlets, and souvenir possibilities range from the grunting "Mr Bacon" pigs at Mag-Neat-O to the wooden salad bowls, turtles, and cannibal forks at Hawaiian Pacific Arts and Crafts. The best of the rest are reviewed below; there's also a Honolua Surf Co (see p.53) and Pipe Dreams Surf Co (see p.54).

Ward Centers

Across from Ala Moana Beach Park and Kewalo Boat Harbor ☎ 808/591-8411, ⓦ www.wardcenters.com. The various Ward malls – the Centre, Warehouse, Farmers Market, Gateway Center, and Village Shops – spread themselves across four blocks along and behind Ala Moana Boulevard, starting a couple of blocks west of the Ala Moana Center. Accessible, like the Ala Moana Center, on both TheBus and the Waikīkī Trolley pink line ($2), this complex, in particular the Ward Centre, has become a serious rival to its bigger neighbor, with a more intimate atmosphere and some distinctive locally owned stores (including a branch of Cinnamon Girl – see p.53 – in the Ward Warehouse).

Shops

Borders Books and Music

Ward Centre ☎ 808/591-8995. Mon–Thurs 9am–11pm, Fri & Sat 9am–midnight, Sun 9am–10pm. The most accessible large book and music store for Waikīkī -based visitors anchors the Ward Centre, stocking lots of local-interest titles, hosting regular music events and author signings. Also has a café.

▼ ALOHA TOWER MARKETPLACE

Compleat Kitchen

Ala Moana Center
☎ 808/944-1741, ⓦ www
.compleatkitchen.com.
Mon–Sat 9.30am–9pm, Sun
10am–7pm. Another branch
in Kahāla Mall (see p.68).
Though the kitchen
implements and utensils
are imported from the
mainland and Europe,
this Hawaiian store is
worth a stop for its
mouthwatering range of
island and Pacific Rim
seasonings, marinades,
and sauces, including
organic ginger honey and
guava butter.

Cottage by the Sea

Ward Warehouse
☎ 808/591-9811, ⓦ www.
cottagehawaii
.com. Mon–Sat 10am–9pm,
Sun 10am–5pm. Airy,
light, and very feminine,
offering a tasteful, well-judged
selection of jewelry, home
furnishings, and gifts, with a
few vintage items dotted for
shabby chic measure. The
handmade sterling silver
bracelets and rings, emblazoned
with inspirational messages,
make good gifts, and are not too
expensive, while the pretty tins
of flower seeds and decoupage
picture frames are a steal.

Hawaiian Ukulele Company

Aloha Tower Marketplace ☎ 808/536-
3228, ⓦ thehawaiianukulelecompany
.com. Mon–Sat 9am–9pm, Sun
9am–6pm. Friendly ukulele shop,
specializing in beautifully crafted
handmade specimens. They stock
the touristy kind, too, brightly
colored and decorated with
hibiscus, but those are cheaper in
the touristy Waikīkī stores. Lots
of vintage ukulele memorabilia,
and occasional on-site lessons.

▲ SOUVENIRS AT HILO HATTIE'S

Hilo Hattie's

Ala Moana Center ☎ 808/973-3266,
ⓦ www.hilohattie.com. Mon–Sat
9.30am–9pm, Sun 10am–7pm.
Hawaii's favorite resort wear
store – a destination in its own
right for busloads of tourists – is
a brash, kitschy place with a
colorful selection of aloha shirts
and sundresses, along with gifts,
souvenirs, books, and CDs. Prices
are good, and it's difficult to leave
without buying something,
whether you're after an aloha tie,
a tiki mug, or a simple pair of
hibiscus-patterned flip flops.

Locals Only

Ala Moana Center ☎ 808/942-1555,
ⓦ www.localsonlyhawaii.com. Mon–Sat
10am–9pm, Sun 10am–6pm. Above-
average aloha shirt store with its
own "Pineapple Juice" brand that
reproduces classic shirt designs
from the 1940s and 50s. They're
made from rayon, which keeps
prices reasonable.

Lupicia

Ala Moana Center ☎808/941-5500.
Mon–Sat 9.30am–9pm, Sun 10am–7pm.
Exquisite Japanese teashop selling a
vast range of loose green, black,
red, white, and flowering teas,
some of them in beautifully
designed gift tins, from around the
world. Tea fanatics will love the
brochures that detail water
temperature, brewing time and
amount of tealeaves for each type.

Mamo Howell

Ward Warehouse ☎808/591-2002,
ⓦwww.mamohowell.com. Mon–Thurs
10am–9pm, Fri & Sat 10am–10pm,
Sun 10am–7pm. Former hula
dancer and fashion model, Mamo
designs tasteful women's *aloha*
wear – sophisticated rather than
splashy – with mumus and formal
long dresses a specialty. Some
equally distinctive men's and
children's styles available.

Native Books/Na Mea Hawaii

Ward Warehouse ☎808/596-8885,
ⓦnativebookshawaii.com. Mon–Thurs
10am–9pm, Fri & Sat 10am–10pm,
Sun 10am–7pm. Another branch of Na
Mea Hawaii in Waikīkī's Hilton
Hawaiian Village. Outstanding store
with locally made crafts – from
tealight holders decorated with
hibiscus to luxuriant *koa* wood
bowls, elaborate shell *leis* and hula
implements – clothing, foodie
gifts, and art. The book selection
is especially good, with a wide
range of titles about Polynesian
history, mythology and art, and
it's a splendid place to buy CDs.
Acting as a community resource,
they host live music Sun 2–4pm,
weekly hula, ukulele, and
Hawaiian language classes, and
occasional art workshops
including lauhala weaving.

Nohea Gallery

Ward Centre ☎808/591-9001; Ward
Warehouse ☎808/596-0074;
ⓦwww.noheagallery.com. Mon–Thurs
10am–9pm, Fri & Sat 10am–10pm,
Sun 10am–7pm. Another branch in
Waikīkī's *Sheraton Moana Surfrider
Hotel.* Original contemporary
artwork, much of it Hawaiian-
themed, from paintings to
ceramics, glasswork, jewelry, and
koa woodcarvings.

Out of the West

Aloha Tower Marketplace ☎808/521-
5552. Mon–Sat 9am–9pm, Sun
9am–6pm. One of the classier
Aloha Tower stores, selling a
range of quirky cowboy-cum-
aloha shirts, mostly for men, but
with a few selections for women,
too. Plus fancy belts, buckles,
bolo ties, cowboy hats, and classic
Tony Lama boots.

Reyn's

Ala Moana Center ☎808/949-5929,
ⓦReyns.com. Mon–Sat 9.30am–9pm,
Sun 10am–7pm. Further branches in
Kahāla Mall (see p.68) and Sheraton
Waikīkī. Reyn's offers distinctive,
limited edition aloha shirts,
designed by a variety of
different artists, made in cotton,
silk, rayon, or seersucker. The
faded "inside-out" reverse-print
designs are favorites, along with
some unbelievably sweet little
cabana outfits (shirt plus shorts)
for kids. Prices can be high for
this "wearable art," so root
around.

Shirokiya

Ala Moana Center ☎808/973-9111,
ⓦwww.shirokiya.com. Mon–Sat
9.30am–9pm, Sun 9.30am–7pm. This
outstanding Japanese department
store is the perfect place to pick
up glorious kimonos, Japanese
ceramics and fabrics, bargain
electronics and intriguing gifts,
all at good prices. Don't miss the
fabulous upstairs food hall, piled
high with sushi, hot noodle
dishes, and *poi.*

▲ JAPANESE DELICACIES AT SHIROKIYA

Restaurants

Chai's Island Bistro

Aloha Tower Marketplace, 101 Ala Moana Blvd ☏808/585-0011, ⓦwww.chaisislandbistro.com. Mon, Sat & Sun 4–10pm; Tues–Fri 11am–10pm.
Beautifully decorated pan-Asian restaurant, half indoors and half out, at the inland side of the Aloha Tower Marketplace. Though it's owned by the same chef as Waikīkī's *Singha Thai* (see p.59), the food can be a bit hit or miss. That's not the main reason to come here, however: *Chai's* books the absolute crème de la crème of Hawaiian musicians to perform live, as detailed on p.98. Miss the show, scheduled for 7–8.30pm, and you'll be paying well over the norm for entrees like *sake* steamed *moi* ($36.95) or grilled Mongolian lamb chops ($37.95). Lunchtimes are cheaper.

E&O Trading Co

Ward Center, Bldg 4, 1200 Ala Moana Blvd ☏808/591-9555, ⓦwww.eotrading.com. Sun–Thurs 11.30am–10.30pm, Fri & Sat 11.30am–11.30pm.
This elegant pan-Asian restaurant, part of a Californian/Hawaiian chain, makes a soothing place to eat when shopping in the Ward Center. Strewn with Indonesian textiles and temple art, it serves similarly eclectic cuisine, with satay (around $7), flat breads ($4–6), and Indonesian corn fritters ($7) sitting next to *char-siu* smoked black cod ($23) and tandoori chicken ($17). Lunch and dinner menus are broadly similar, though lunch is a little cheaper, with a few specials for $13 – Korean BBQ beef or firecracker chicken stir-fried with asparagus, for example – and they offer a couple more entrees at night.

Gordon Biersch Brewery Restaurant

Aloha Tower Marketplace, 101 Ala Moana Blvd ☏808/599-4877. Mon–Thurs & Sun 10am–10pm, Fri & Sat 10am–11pm; bar open until midnight Mon–Thurs & Sun, 1am Fri & Sat.
This chain brewpub offers one of Aloha Tower's more stylish options, with seating either outdoors on a large dockside terrace, or indoors, near a long bar that's brimming with beers from around the globe. For lunch ($9–16) try a pizza, a goat cheese and hummus salad, a burger or grill item, or the cashew chicken stir-fry. The dinner menu offers the same pizzas and salads, Hawaiian regional dishes such as sesame seared *ahi* ($22.50), plus Japanese and Thai-tinged choices. Live music Wed–Sat evenings.

▲ HIROSHI EURASIAN TAPAS

Waterfront Honolulu

PLACES

Waterfront Honolulu

Hiroshi Eurasian Tapas

Restaurant Row, 500 Ala Moana Blvd
☎808/533-4476, ⓦwww
.dkrestaurants.com. Daily
5.30–9.30pm. Anyone familiar with
Spanish-style dining shouldn't
expect to find the same experience
here; though they profess to offer
small plates of food "designed for
sharing", these are more like
largish appetizers, and prices ($7–
16) mean that costs easily mount
up. As you would expect from the
people who brought you the
superlative *Sansei* restaurants, the
food, combining Mediterranean
and pan-Asian cuisines – foie gras
sushi, truffled crab cake, miso
butterfish, Portuguese sausage
potfillers – is across
the board delicious,
and the atmosphere
smart, contemporary,
and vibrant. Larger
plates – *onaga* with
cauliflower purée,
wilted *tatsoi* and fresh
basil, for example –
cost between $20 and
$28.

Kaka'ako Kitchen

Ward Center, 1200 Ala
Moana Blvd ☎808/596-
7488. Mon–Thurs
7–10am & 10.30am–
9pm, Fri 7–10am &
10.30am–10pm,
Sat 7–11am & 11.30am–10pm, Sun
7–11am & 11.30am–5pm. Cheery
mall restaurant that dishes up
gourmet home-cooking,
Hawaiian-style. The presentation
is no-frills – after ordering at the
counter, you eat with plastic
cutlery from styrofoam boxes –
but the food is healthy and
excellent. Everything, from the
char siu pork salad through the
tempura catfish to the island-style
chicken linguine, costs $7–10,
with daily specials for carnivores
(meat loaf, pot roast, curry) and
veggies (stir-fry tofu, eggplant
parmesan) alike. Breakfast options
include *mahi mahi* with eggs for
$7.25. Credit cards accepted for
checks of $50 and over only.

La Mariana Sailing Club

50 Sand Island Access Rd ☎808/848-
2800. Daily 11am–3pm & 5–9pm. An
atmospheric old-time restaurant
– technically a "yacht club" – on
a very obscure stretch of
Honolulu's industrial waterfront.
The decor, which crosses original
1950s cocktail lounge styling
with South Seas thrift store
kitsch, is the real thing, and the
ambience – created by a mixed
crowd of eccentric locals and

▼ KAKA'AKO KITCHEN

in-the-know tourists – slightly
surreal. Hearty fish appetizers
like *taco poke* (marinated octopus)
cost between $6 and $13, while
full dinners such as seafood
brochette or *ahi* Cajun go for
under $20. The food isn't the
main draw here, however – try
and time your visit to coincide
with the impromptu live
Hawaiian music on Friday
evenings, from 6pm until 9pm;
for more details, see p.98.

L'Uraku

1341 Kapi'olani Blvd ☎808/955-0552,
🌐www.luraku.com. Daily 11am–2pm
& 5.30–10pm. Quirky, hip Japanese
restaurant on a busy street a block
inland from the Ala Moana mall.
The interior is festooned with
crudely hand-painted umbrellas
that trace the saga of a lost
Somalian cat. Most of the menu
is solidly Japanese, but there's a
strong Italian flavor as well,
including a daily pasta special.
Delicious appetizers, ranging
from a single baked oyster ($2.50)
up to a bento box filled with
goodies ($13), are matched by
entrees ($16–28) that include
steamed fish and garlic steak. A
dinner "tasting" menu is $34 ($47
with wine), while at lunchtime
on weekends they offer a bargain
$16 set meal.

OnJin's Cafe

401 Kamake'e St ☎808/589-1666.
Mon–Sat 11am–10pm, Sun
11am–9pm. Bright, smart little
café, one block inland from the
Ward Center, offering quality
cooking at very reasonable prices.
At lunchtime, when orders are
taken at the counter, pretty much
everything costs $7.50–10 – and
that includes the crispy snapper
in lemon beurre blanc ($8.25),
and the daily specials like
Thursday's roast leg of lamb, as
well as wraps, burgers, and

▲ LA MARIANA SAILING CLUB

PLACES Waterfront Honolulu

sandwiches. The service is more
formal in the evening, and the
prices are significantly higher,
with entrees such as half a duck
in Grand Marnier for $18.50, and
bouillabaisse for $24.

Sam Choy's Breakfast, Lunch and Crab

580 N Nimitz Hwy ☎808/545-7979,
🌐www.samchoy.com. Restaurant
Mon–Thurs 7am–3pm & 5–9.30pm,
Fri & Sat 7am–4pm & 5–10pm, Sun
7am–4pm & 5–9.30pm; brewery daily
10.30am until late. *Sam Choy's
Diamond Head* is reviewed on p.69. A
mile or two west of downtown,
tightly sandwiched between the
west- and east-bound sides of the
Nimitz Highway, this garish
Hawaiian diner looks unenticing
from the outside. Inside, though,
you'll find a full-sized sampan
fishing boat, the gleaming *Big
Aloha* microbrewery, and crowds
of diners eager to gorge on
celebrity chef Choy's trademark
local cuisine. Crab is a feature, of
course, along with hefty
breakfasts (from $6) – go for the
Hawaiian specialties, like *kālua*
pork *loco moco* – and plate lunches

($9–15) that come very big indeed – the fried *poke* ($12) is a must. Evening entrees ($18–30), include fresh fish, paella, crabs' legs, and roasted or steamed whole crabs and lobsters.

Bars and clubs

Ocean club

Restaurant Row, 500 Ala Moana Blvd ☎808/531-8444, ⓦwww .oceanclubonline.com. Tues–Fri 4.30pm–4am, Sat 7pm–4am. Big, loud, and very glitzy bar/ nightclub that's a major hangout for downtown's after-work crowd and won't admit anyone wearing a T-shirt or under 23 years old (except Thurs, when ages 21 & 22 are also welcome). The short menu of seafood snacks like crab dip and sashimi is half-price before 8pm; after that, there's a $5 cover charge, and the dancing continues late into the night.

Pipeline

805 Pohukaina St, Honolulu ☎808/589-1999, ⓦwww.pipelinecafe .net. Mon–Thurs 9pm–4am, Fri & Sat 10pm–4am. Just behind the Ala Moana mall, this is a favorite with the surf set, who come for DJ music most nights, and perhaps one rock or reggae gig per week (the only time there's a cover charge). Door policy varies nightly between over-20s and over-17s; call to check.

Rumours

Ala Moana Hotel, 410 Atkinson Drive, Honolulu ☎808/955-4811. Thurs 5pm–2am, Fri 5pm–4am, Sat 9pm–4am. Mainstream, old-style disco in a business hotel behind the Ala Moana mall. Extremely popular with the after-work local crowd. Friday's 70s night is a fixture on many calendars.

Live music venues

Chai's Island Bistro

Aloha Tower Marketplace, 101 Ala Moana Blvd ☎808/585-0011. Sumptuous and very expensive Thai restaurant, which books the very finest Hawaiian musicians to perform nightly 7–8.30pm. The precise schedule varies, but currently includes long-term residencies by Sista Robi Kahakalau (Sun), Robert Cazimero (Tues), the Brothers Cazimero (Wed), and regular appearances by one or both members of Hapa. For a full review, see p.95.

La Mariana Sailing Club

50 Sand Island Access Rd ☎808/848-2800. Atmospheric and extremely quirky waterfront restaurant – the food is reviewed on p.96 – with an authentic 1950s ambience, hidden away amid the docks of Honolulu. The week's high point is Friday evening, from 8.30pm onwards, when pianist Ron Miyashiro and a group of semi-professional singers work their way through a nostalgic set of classic Hawaiian songs, but there's also live piano music nightly except Mon 5–9pm. Don't miss – it's practically the last of a dying breed. No cover.

Makiki and Mānoa

The more time you spend in Honolulu, the more your eyes are likely to stray toward the mysterious mountains that soar just a short distance inland, and the valleys that lie between them. Many former wilderness areas have been colonized by residential developments, but there's still plenty of pristine rainforest within easy reach of downtown, waiting to be explored along spectacular hiking trails. In addition, the few roads that wind through the hills also hold some notable city landmarks, including Punchbowl cemetery.

Tantalus and Round Top drives and around

For a quick escape into Honolulu's hilly hinterland, there's no better route than Tantalus and Round Top drives. They're actually a single eight-mile road that climbs up one flanking ridge of Makiki Valley and then wriggles back down the other, changing its name from Tantalus Drive in the west to Round Top Drive in the east. Along the way through what's known as Makiki Heights, you'll get plenty of views of Honolulu and Waikīkī , but the real attraction is the dense rainforest

that cloaks the hillside. It's a slow drive, which in places narrows to just a single lane of traffic, but a spellbinding one.

It's also possible to skip the bulk of the circuit by taking Makiki Heights Drive, which holds the stimulating Contemporary Museum as well as trailheads for some superb mountain hikes.

Further southeast, Mānoa may lie just a couple of miles from Waikīkī – it's directly inland, to the north – but it's light-years away from the commercial hustle of the city. Behind the University of Hawaii a quiet residential suburb peters out as it narrows

▼ VIEW FROM PUNCHBOWL

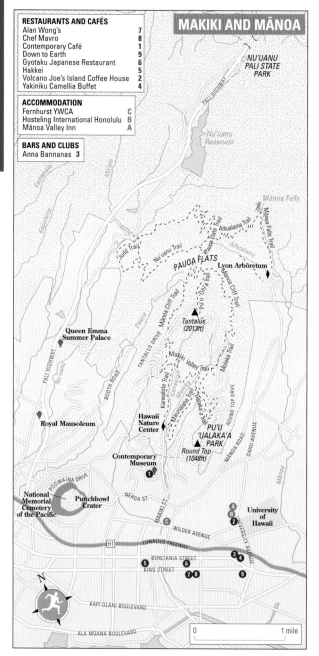

RESTAURANTS AND CAFÉS

Alan Wong's	7
Chef Mavro	8
Contemporary Café	1
Down to Earth	9
Gyotaku Japanese Restaurant	6
Hakkei	5
Volcano Joe's Island Coffee House	2
Yakiniku Camellia Buffet	4

ACCOMMODATION

Fernhurst YWCA	C
Hosteling International Honolulu	B
Mānoa Valley Inn	A

BARS AND CLUBS

Anna Bannanas	3

MAKIKI AND MĀNOA

into the mountains, culminating at the back end of Mānoa Valley in a spectacular tropical waterfall.

Punchbowl: National Memorial Cemetery of the Pacific

March–Sept daily 8am–6.30pm; Oct–Feb daily 8am–5.30pm; admission free. Perched above downtown Honolulu, the extinct volcanic caldera known as Punchbowl makes an evocative setting for the National Memorial Cemetery of the Pacific. To ancient Hawaiians, this was Pūowaina, the hill of human sacrifices; somewhere within its high encircling walls stood a sacrificial temple. It's now possible to drive right into the crater – having first spiralled around the base of the cone to meet up with Pūowaina Drive from the back – and park in one of the many small bays dotted around the perimeter road.

Beneath the lawns that carpet the bowl-shaped interior, well over 25,000 dead of US Pacific wars, and also Vietnam, now lie buried. Famous names here also include the Hawaiian astronaut Ellison Onizuka, killed when the *Challenger* shuttle exploded, but no graves are singled out for special attention. Instead, each gravestone, marked perhaps with a bouquet of ginger and heliconia, is recessed into the grass, with space left for their families or still-living veterans to join those laid to rest. Opposite the entrance rises the imposing marble staircase of the Honolulu Memorial, where ten "Courts of the Missing" commemorate a further 28,778 service personnel listed as missing in action. It culminates in a thirty-foot marble relief of the prow of a naval ship.

Only when you climb the footpath to the top of the crater rim and find yourself looking straight down Punchbowl Street to the Capitol do you appreciate how close this all is to downtown Honolulu. During World War II, before the creation of the cemetery, this ridge held heavy artillery trained out to sea.

Contemporary Museum

2411 Makiki Heights Drive. Tues–Sat 10am–4pm, Sun noon–4pm; $5, free on the third Thurs of every month, under-13s free; ☎808/526-1322, ⊛www.tcmhi.org. At 2411 Makiki Heights Drive, a short distance east of that road's intersection with Mott-Smith Drive, a grand 1920s country estate houses the lovely Contemporary Museum. The

▼ NATIONAL MEMORIAL CEMETERY (PUNCHBOWL)

▲ DOG STATUE AT THE CONTEMPORARY MUSEUM

Contemporary Museum, or half a mile west of the intersection with Makiki Street. Follow the dead-end road to park in a large lot on its left side, just beyond a sign that announces you've entered the Makiki Forest Recreation Area.

Walking a little further on from here will bring you to the ramshackle green trailers of the Hawaii Nature Center (☏808/955-0100, Ⓦwww.hawaiinaturecenter .org), a volunteer educational group that works mainly with schoolchildren and organizes guided hikes, open to all, on weekends. However, to take the best loop trip from this point, you don't need to go as far as the Nature Center. Set off instead across the Kanealole Stream, which flows parallel to the road on its right-hand side, on the clearly signed Maunalaha Trail. A short way up, you'll come to a T-junction, with the Kanealole Trail arrowed to the left and the Maunalaha to the right. Follow the Maunalaha, and you swiftly switchback on to the ridge for a long straight climb, often stepping from one exposed tree root to the next. Despite being in the shade most of the way, it's a grueling haul. Looking back through the deep green woods, you'll glimpse the towers of downtown Honolulu and then of Waikīkī. At first you can see the valleys to either side of the ridge, but before long only Mānoa Valley to the east is visible. After roughly three-quarters of a mile, you come to a four-way intersection at the top of the hill.

This is the point to decide just how far you want to walk. The shortest route back to the

grounds are tastefully landscaped with ornamental Oriental gardens that offer a superb overview of Honolulu and are packed with playful sculptures, while the museum itself is really more of an art gallery than a museum, and hosts changing exhibitions of up-to-the-minute fine art. Few last more than eight weeks, but each is installed with lavish attention to detail.

A separate pavilion houses a permanent display of the sets created by David Hockney for the Metropolitan Opera's production of Ravel's *L'Enfant et les Sortilèges*, accompanied by a recording of the work playing constantly. Excellent lunches are available at the on-site Contemporary Café (see p.107), and there's also a very good gift store.

Makiki Valley trails

Honolulu's finest hiking trails wind their way across and around the slopes of Makiki Valley. The network is most easily accessed via a short spur road that leads inland from a hairpin bend in Makiki Heights Drive, roughly half a mile east of the

▲ KANEALOLE TRAIL SIGN

trailhead is simply to return the way you came, while turning left here, onto the Makiki Valley Trail, will enable you to complete a highly recommended loop hike of 2.5 miles. The first stretch of the Makiki Valley Trail is the most gorgeous of the lot. A gentle descent angled along the steep valley wall, it heads inland to cross Moleka Stream at Herring Springs, amid a profusion of tiny bright flowers. Climbing away again you're treated to further ravishing views of the high valley, bursting with bright gingers and fruit trees. Birds are audible all around, and dangling lianas festoon the path. Take Kanealole Trail, which cuts away to the left shortly before this trail meets Tantalus Drive, and you'll drop back down through endless guava trees to your starting point near the Nature Center.

Alternatively, you can head right at the four-way intersection described above, and take the 'Ualaka'a Trail, to add an enjoyable if muddy half-mile to the loop trip. Plunging into the forest, the level path soon passes some extraordinary banyans, perched on the steep slopes with their many trunks, which have engulfed older trees. Having rounded the ridge, where a magnificent avenue of Cook pines marches along the crest in parallel rows, an arm-span apart, you curve back to cross Round Top Drive twice. In between the two crossings, take the short spur trail that leads left and up to the highest point on the hike. A clearing here perfectly frames Diamond Head against the ocean, with Waikīkī to the right of Diamond Head and the gleaming silver dome of the sports stadium at the University of Hawaii straight below. Once you rejoin the main trail on the far side of Round Top Drive – it starts fifty yards to the right – a brief woodland walk, down to the left, returns you to the four-way junction.

Finally, it's also possible to continue straight ahead from the four-way intersection. As first the Moleka Trail, and subsequently the Mānoa Cliff Trail, this route brings you in roughly three miles to the Nu'uanu Pali Lookout, described on p.112. You're now almost four miles from your car, so you have a total hike of around eight miles.

Tantalus trails

Tantalus Drive is at its highest just below the 2013-foot pinnacle of Tantalus itself, near the point where it changes its name to Round Top Drive. Two roadside parking lots here stand close to the trailhead for the three-quarter-mile Pu'u 'Ōhi'a Trail. The initial climb up through the eucalyptus trees to the summit is steep enough to require the aid of a wooden staircase, which comes out after a few hundred yards onto a little-used paved track. Follow this to the right until you reach a fenced-off electrical substation, then cut down the footpath to the left, which leads through a dense grove of bamboo before veering right to join the Mānoa Cliff Trail. By now you'll have seen the vastness of Nu'uanu Valley extending away to your left; heading left brings you, in a couple of hundred yards, to the Pauoa Flats Trail. As that in turn heads for three quarters of a mile into the valley, it's met first by the Nu'uanu Trail from the west, and then by the Aihualama Trail from Mānoa Falls (see opposite) from the east.

The Pauoa Flats Trail ends at a vantage point poised high above Nu'uanu Valley, though for even more dramatic views you can double back slightly and climb the knife-edge ridge to your left, from where it's obvious how Nu'uanu Valley cuts right through the heart of Oahu. Down below the lookout, the Nu'uanu Reservoir is an artificial lake that's kept stocked with crayfish and catfish; fishing is only permitted on three weekends in the year.

Pu'u 'Ualaka'a Park

The single best view along Round Top Drive comes at Pu'u 'Ualaka'a Park, on the western flank of Mānoa Valley. There's not much of a park here, though there's a sheltered hilltop picnic pavilion at the first of its two parking lots. Continue beyond that to the second lot, however, where a paved walkway leads to a railed-off viewing area right at the end of the ridge, and you'll be rewarded with a panorama of the entire southern coast of Oahu. The twin craters of Diamond Head to the left and Punchbowl to the right most readily draw the eye, but looking away to the west you can see

beyond the airport and Pearl Harbor and all the way to Barber's Point. Pools of glittering glass in the parking lot attest to the many break-ins up here, so don't spend too long away from your vehicle.

The small summit that separates the two lots is Round Top itself. The Hawaiians called it 'Ualaka'a ("rolling sweet potato"), because Kamehameha the Great decreed the planting of sweet potatoes here, which when dug up rolled down the hillside.

University of Hawaii

The main campus of the University of Hawaii sprawls along University Avenue in Mānoa, bounded on its southern side by H-1, Honolulu's major east–west freeway. Courses at the University focus largely on its specialties of geology, marine studies, astronomy, and other Pacific-related fields. While a magnet for students from around the Pacific, it holds no great appeal for casual visitors. Furthermore, only a tiny proportion of students live on campus, so there are fewer stores, restaurants, and clubs in the vicinity than you might expect. The Campus Center, set a little way back from University Avenue, is the place to head for general information and orientation. Hemenway Hall alongside holds the inexpensive, weekday-only *Mānoa Garden* café, as well as a movie theater.

Lyon Arboretum

3860 Mānoa Road. Mon–Fri 9am–4pm; free; ☎808/988-0456, ⓦwww.hawaii .edu/lyonarboretum. The Lyon Arboretum guards the approaches to the uppermost reaches of Mānoa Valley. To drive there, continue along University Avenue beyond the campus, cross

E Mānoa Road onto Oahu Avenue, and then turn right onto Mānoa Road itself. Immediately you'll see the silver stream of Mānoa Falls amid the trees at the head of the valley. Mānoa Road comes to a halt just beyond the Arboretum itself, which belongs to the University and preserves Hawaiian and imported trees in a reasonable approximation of their native environment. Several short trails crisscross beneath the canopy.

Mānoa Falls

At three-quarters of a mile each way, the round-trip hike to Mānoa Falls, towering 160 feet high at the head of Mānoa Valley, is the most rewarding and enjoyable short trail on Oahu. Considering how close it is to the heart of Honolulu, it offers a quite amazing sense of delving deep into a gorgeous tropical rainforest. Expect to spend around an hour and a half away from your vehicle, and don't wait to get bitten before you cover yourself with mosquito repellent.

Signs posted all around the end of the road, beyond the Arboretum, warn drivers not to park illegally. The area is notorious for break-ins, so it's unwise to leave valuables in your car. The one place you clearly *can* park is in the large lot of the defunct Paradise Park, where there's usually an attendant to collect the $5 fee.

The trail to the falls follows straight on ahead. Having passed over a footbridge and through a soggy meadow, it soon starts to climb beside one of the two main tributaries of Mānoa Stream. After scrambling from root to protruding root, over intertwined banyans and bamboos, you come out at the soaring high falls, where the flat, mossy cliff face is at enough of an angle that the water flows rather than falls into the small pool at its base. Sadly, thanks to recent landslides, access to the foot of the falls is strictly forbidden.

Many hikers combine the trek to the falls with tackling the much more demanding Aihualama Trail. That switchbacks steeply up to the west from an inconspicuous intersection just short of the falls. After something over a mile, it comes out on top of the ridge, amid a thick cluster of bamboo, to connect with the Makiki network of trails half a mile short

▼ MĀNOA FALLS

of the Nuʻuanu Pali Lookout (see p.112).

Shops

The Contemporary Museum Store

2411 Makiki Heights Drive ☎808/523-3447, ⓦwww.tcmhi.org. Tues–Sat 10am–4pm, Sun noon–4pm. Whacky, eccentric, kitsch, and arty is the name of the game here, with everything from mini heart-shaped water bottles to surreal Japanese prints for sale. The museum is covered on p.101.

Rainbow Books & Records

1010 University Ave at King St ☎808/955-7994. Mon–Thurs & Sun 10am–10pm, Fri & Sat 10am–11pm. There's an amazing amount of stuff to read and listen to crammed into this tiny hole-in-the-wall store near the University, including a good Hawaiiana section.

Cafés

Volcano Joe's Island Coffee House

1810 University Ave ☎808/941-8449, ⓦwww.volcanojoes.com. Coffeehouse Mon–Fri 6am–8pm, Sat & Sun 7am–8pm; bistro daily 11am–10pm. Across the street from the university campus, and handy to the Honolulu International Hostel (see p.173), this casual café is a convenient stop-off on the way to or from Mānoa Falls. Breakfast includes waffles and pastries, while lunch and dinner ($5–8) revolves around wraps, gourmet pizza, salads, and vegan specials. Local up-and-coming bands play on Monday evenings; BYOB.

Restaurants

Alan Wong's

1857 S King St ☎808/949-2526, ⓦwww.alanwongs.com. Daily 5–10pm. Though expensive and hard to find – it's tucked away on the third floor in a nondescript area southwest of the University – *Alan Wong's* is one of Honolulu's most fashionable gourmet rendezvous, thanks to its fantastic contemporary Hawaiian cuisine. Besides changing daily specials, appetizers always include the signature "da bag," a giant foil bag holding clams steamed with *kālua* pig, shiitake mushrooms,

▼ VOLCANO JOE'S

and spinach ($11.50), and "poki-pines," crispy *ahi poke* won tons with avocado and wasabi ($15). Typical entrees ($26–52) include ginger-crusted *onaga* (snapper) and oil-poached lamb rib-eye with three sauces. There's always something new and delicious to try: nightly tasting menus cost $75 (five courses) and $95 (seven courses). Valet parking only.

Chef Mavro

1969 S King St ☏ 808/944-4714, ⊛ www.chefmavro.com. Daily except Mon 6–9.30pm. Greek-born chef George Mavrothalassitis stands out in Honolulu's gourmet dining scene for his seasonally changing prix-fixe menus (three courses $65, $98 with a different wine for each course; four courses $71/$115; six courses $102/$150), and his eleven-course "degustation" menu for four ($150/$212). The menu sounds fussy – roasted loin of kurobuta pork with sansho jus, apple quinoa, and savoy cabbage gribiche, say, or kobe-style roasted bavette and braised short rib with pancetta Brussels sprouts, truffle-accented celery root purée, and Pinot Noir sauce – but the food itself, a fusion of nouvelle contemporary Hawaiian, is delicate and delightful.

Contemporary Café

Contemporary Museum, 2411 Makiki Heights Drive ☏ 808/523-3362. Tues–Sat 11.30am–2.30pm, Sun noon–2.30pm. Excellent lunches, with soups, salads, and daily specials like tofu burgers or vegetable bruschetta priced at $10–12.

Down to Earth

2525 S King St ☏ 808/947-7678. Daily 7.30am–9pm. Long-standing natural food store near the University. The inexpensive deli counter offers a full vegetarian menu including curries, baked pies, and pastas – some with tofu, some with cheese – plus sandwiches, salads and wraps, fresh fruit smoothies, and juices.

Gyotaku Japanese Restaurant

1824 S King St ☏ 808/949-4584. Bento take out daily 9.30am–2.30pm; restaurant Sun–Thurs 11am–9pm, Fri & Sat 11am–10pm. During the day, this is a hotspot for locals grabbing bento boxes – butterfish, teriyaki beef, tempura – for around $7. The sit-down dining room offers more bento, as well as a fine range of sushi and sashimi and tempting noodles, *wa-zen*, and *kamameshi*, from $12. The *poke don teishoku* ($14.95) is particularly tasty, with the fresh *poke* served over rice. No reservations.

Hakkei

1436 Young St ☏ 808/944-6688, ⊛ www.hakkei-honolulu.com. Daily except Tues 11.30am–2pm & 5.30–11pm. Specializing in *washoku* cuisine, with unfussy dishes like *oden* (a flavorful hotpot cooked with anything from turnips and pumpkin to tofu and Japanese fish cake), crispy rice, home-made pickled vegetables and fresh veggies. The daily lunch specials – deep-fried butterfish, mushroom, and soybean hotpot, scallop *kamameshi* – provide the best value.

Yakiniku Camellia Buffet

2494 S Beretania St ☏ 808/946-7955. Daily 10.30am–10pm. Authentic, cheap and cheerful Korean buffet restaurant about a mile north of Waikīkī, just south of the University. The few non-Korean speakers who venture in have to fend for themselves, joining families and hungry locals heaping their plates again and again. Whether at lunch ($12) or dinner ($19), the food is a treat;

you select slices of marinated beef, chicken, or pork from refrigerated cabinets and grill them yourself at the gas-fired burners set into each table. There are also lots of vegetables, as well as a wide assortment of super-fresh salads, including octopus, seaweed, *ahi poke*, pickles, and delicious tiny dried fish.

Bars

Anna Banannas
2440 S Beretania St ☎808/946-5190. Daily 9pm–2am. University district bar with reasonable prices, live R&B and reggae most nights, and a hectic weekend atmosphere.

The Pali and Likelike Highways

In ancient times, the Koʻolau Mountains constituted an impassable obstacle between Honolulu and windward Oahu. Early tourists rode to the 3000-foot ridge atop Nuʻuanu Valley, but there was no way to get down the far side. These days, three separate roads cross the mountains – the Pali and Likelike (pronounced *leek-e-leek-e*) highways, and the H-3 freeway.

High-speed traffic thunders along the Pali Highway day and night, but it remains attractive nonetheless, and at several points you can detour onto peaceful stretches. Likelike Highway is less spectacular. Starting two miles west, it runs through residential Kalihi Valley before passing through its own tunnel to emerge just above Kāneʻohe. There's no great reason to cross the island this way, but it does provide access to Honolulu's best museum, the Bishop Museum. H-3, meanwhile, serves primarily as a commuter route and is of minimal significance for tourists.

The Royal Mausoleum

2261 Nuʻuanu Avenue. Mon–Fri 8am–4pm; free. The Gothic-influenced Royal Mausoleum is located very near the top of Nuʻuanu Avenue, shortly before it joins the Pali Highway. It would be very easy to miss – there's no sign, so watch out on the right as soon as you've passed the Japanese cemetery – and frankly it's not worth losing any sleep if you do.

The drab, gray mausoleum itself, built in 1865 to replace the overcrowded Kamehameha family tomb at ʻIolani Palace, stands at the end of a short oval driveway ringed with lumpy palm trees. It's now simply a chapel, as the bodies it

▼ ROYAL MAUSOLEUM

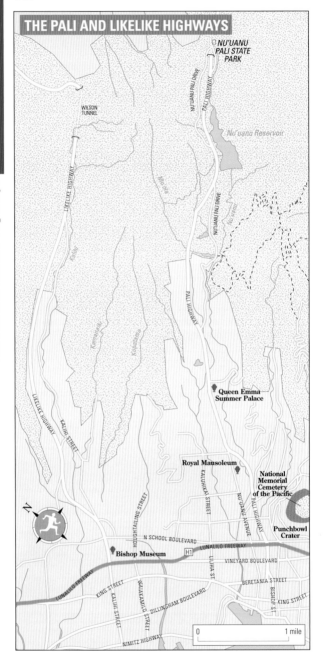

held for its first forty years or so were later moved to various sarcophagi dotted around the lawns. Kamehameha the Great was buried in secret on the Big Island, but most of his closest family, as Christians, now lie here. His widow Ka'ahumanu, along with Kamehamehas II to V, are in the pink granite tomb to the left, while members of the separate Kalākaua dynasty were reinterred in the gilded vault beneath the central black column. Incidentally, this spot is said to be the precise site where the Nu'uanu Valley battle began in 1795.

Queen Emma Summer Palace

2913 Pali Hwy. Daily 9am–4pm; adults $6, under-12s $1; ☎808/595-3167, ⓦwww.daughtersofhawaii.org. A couple of miles up the Pali Highway, just over half a mile after its intersection with Nu'uanu Avenue, a former royal retreat stands on the brow of a small hill to the right of the road. The Queen Emma Summer Palace made a welcome escape from the heat of Honolulu for the former Emma Rooke, who

married King Kamehameha IV in 1856, was queen consort until 1863, and lived here until her death in 1885. It's now run as a somewhat cloying shrine to her memory.

Behind its entrance stairway and six Doric pillars, the single-story white frame house is surprisingly small. Guided tours proceed at a snail's pace through rooms lined with royal souvenirs; only the splendidly grumpy Princess Ruth relieves the monotony of the official portraits. Among touching memorabilia of the young Prince Albert Edward – Queen Emma's only child, who died aged 4 – are his beautiful koa-wood crib, carved to resemble a canoe rocked by the waves, and a fireman's outfit he once wore in a parade. Gifts from Queen Victoria, after whose husband the boy was named, make up a large proportion of the items on display. Both Victoria and Emma were widowed – Emma was only 27 when her husband died a year after their son – and the two women continued to exchange presents for the rest of their lives.

▼ QUEEN EMMA'S SUMMER PALACE

▲ NU'UANU PALI STATE PARK

Nu'uanu Pali State Park

Daily 4am–8pm; free. A right turn half a mile up the Pali Highway beyond Queen Emma's palace leads onto Nu'uanu Pali Drive, an appealing side road into the rainforest which rejoins the highway after something over a mile. It's the *next* right turn after that, another mile along and once more labeled as Nu'uanu Pali Drive, that you should really be looking out for, as it offers your one chance to enjoy the staggering overview of the cliffs of windward Oahu from Nu'uanu Pali State Park. At the edge of a small parking lot here, the railed viewing area of the Nu'uanu Pali Lookout is perched near the top of a magnificent curtain of green velvet, plunging more than a thousand feet. Straight ahead lie the sprawling coastal communities of Kailua and Kāne'ohe, separated by the Mōkapu Peninsula, but your eye is likely to be drawn to the north, where the mighty *pali* seems to stretch away forever, with a waterfall in every fold.

It was over this fearsome drop that the defeated warriors of Oahu were driven in 1795;

The Battle of Nu'uanu Valley

For early foreign visitors, the ride to the top of Nu'uanu Pali was an essential part of a Hawaiian itinerary. As their horses struggled up, native guides would recount tales of the epic **Battle of Nu'uanu Valley** in 1795, in which Kamehameha the Great (from the Big Island) defeated Kalanikūpule and conquered the island of Oahu.

Kamehameha's army landed at Honolulu to find Kalanikūpule waiting for them in Nu'uanu Valley. Kamehameha sent men along the tops of the ridges to either side, and advanced towards Kalanikūpule in the center himself. His entourage included not only Europeans but, crucially, a few European guns. Isaac Davis, who five years previously had been the sole survivor of a Hawaiian raid on the Big Island, positioned himself at the front of the attack.

Before the usual ritual of challenges and counter-challenges could even begin, Davis killed Kalanikūpule's leading general with a single lucky shot. The soldiers of Oahu turned tail and ran, pursued all the way to the head of the valley. When they reached the top, where the thousand-foot Nu'uanu Pali precipice drops away on the far side, they had no choice. Almost to a man, they hurtled to their deaths. Kalanikūpule managed to hide out in Oahu's mountains for several months, before he was captured and sacrificed to Kamehameha's personal war god.

placards at the overlook explain the course of the battle and point out assorted landmarks. An estimated four hundred skulls were found down below when the Pali Highway was built a century later. The stairs that head down to the right lead to the highway's original route as it edges its way above the precipice. It's blocked off about a mile along, but walking to the end makes a good, if windy, mountain hike.

If you're heading across the island, you have to drive back down to rejoin the highway where you left it. To the right, Nuʻuanu Pali Drive crosses over a tunnel and meets the highway's other carriageway on the far side, to drop back into Honolulu.

Bishop Museum

1525 Bernice St. Daily 9am–5pm; adults $14.95, ages 4–12 and seniors $11.95; prices include the planetarium; planetarium shows daily 11am & 2pm, plus 7pm Fri & Sat, admission to planetarium alone $4.50; ☎808/847 -3511, ⓦwww.bishopmuseum.org.

The best museum of Hawaiian history, anthropology, and natural history – and the world's finest collection of the arts of the Pacific – is located in the largely residential Kahili neighborhood, two miles northwest of downtown Honolulu. To reach the Bishop Museum, catch TheBus #2 from Waikīkī or drive to the foot of Likelike Highway and follow the signs from the first exit on the right.

The museum spreads across four main buildings on a twelve-acre hillside estate. The first section you come to, past the ticket hall, is Hawaii's only planetarium, while the original core of the museum beyond that houses the bulk of its historic displays. At the time this book

▼ MASKS AT THE BISHOP MUSEUM

went to press, its grand Hawaiian Hall was closed for renovations, but it's expected to reopen with many of the same exhibits as before. Several of its most treasured ancient artifacts remain on display, including Kamehameha the Great's personal wooden effigy of the war god Kūkā'ilimoku, found in a cave in Kona on the Big Island, and a crested feather helmet that probably belonged to Kalaniopu'u of the Big Island.

The adjoining Polynesian Hall, not affected by the renovations, emphasizes the full diversity of Polynesia. Stunning exhibits here include woven-grass masks and dance costumes from Vanikoro, modeled skulls and figures from Vanuato, stark white and red sorcery charms from Papua New Guinea, and stick charts used by Micronesian navigators.

In the Castle Building next door, you'll find top-quality temporary exhibitions, while the new Science Adventure Center holds very lavish, high-tech displays on earth and life sciences, aimed largely at local schoolchildren. Its centerpiece is an enormous artificial volcano, which constantly "erupts" fountains of glowing orange liquid. The Bishop Museum holds an excellent bookstore as well as a snack bar.

Shops

Shop Pacifica

Bishop Museum, 1525 Bernice St ☎808/848-4156, ⓦwww .bishopmuseum.org. Daily 9am–5pm. Besides the obvious learned books and treatises (many of them published by the museum's own press), this quirky and enjoyable shop stocks a great range of Hawaiian crafts, clothing, jewelry, and gifts – even "mongoose" (as opposed to mouse) pads for your computer. Pretty much everything is also available online.

Pearl Harbor

Ancient Hawaiians knew the vast inlet of Pearl Harbor, reaching deep into the heart of Oahu, as *Wai Momi*, "water of pearl," on account of its pearl-bearing oysters. Today, the 12,600-acre Pearl Harbor Naval Complex is the headquarters from which the US Pacific Fleet patrols just over a hundred million square miles of ocean. The entire fleet consists of approximately two hundred ships, two thousand aircraft and 239,000 personnel, while Pearl Harbor itself is the home port for around twelve surface vessels and sixteen nuclear submarines.

Except for the offshore Arizona Memorial, commemorating the surprise Japanese attack with which Pearl Harbor remains synonymous, almost the whole area is off limits to civilians.

USS Arizona Memorial

Visitor center open daily 7.30am–5pm; Day, tours 8am–3pm; closed New Year's, Thanksgiving, & Christmas Day; free; ☎808/422-0561, ⓦwww.nps.gov/usar. Almost half the victims of the December 1941 Japanese attack on Pearl Harbor were aboard the battleship *USS Arizona*. Hit by an armor-piercing shell that detonated its magazine and lifted its bow twenty feet out of the water, it sank within nine minutes. Of its 1514 crew members – who had earned the right to sleep in late that Sunday morning by coming second in a military band competition – 1177 were killed.

The *Arizona* still lies submerged where it came to rest, out in the waters of the harbor along "Battleship Row," next to Ford Island. Its wreck is spanned (though not touched) by the curving white Arizona Memorial, maintained by the National Park Service in

▲ PEARL HARBOR VISITOR CENTER

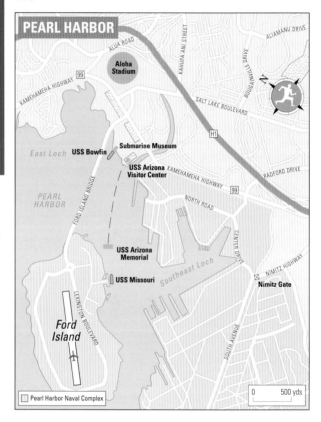

honor of all the victims of the attack; small boats ferry a stream of visitors out from the mainland.

The visitor center for the memorial is located six miles west of Honolulu, just over a mile after Kamehameha Highway cuts off to the left of H-1. It takes up to an hour to drive across town from Waikīkī; the large warning signs that you'll see as you approach, restricting admission to the naval base, don't apply to memorial visitors. TheBus #20 runs direct from Waikīkī, as do overpriced commercial tours (typically around $25 per person, with the operators listed on p.183). No reservations are accepted, so each individual has to pick up his or her own numbered ticket for the free memorial tour on arrival. The average wait is around ninety minutes, while in peak season it can easily be two or three hours before you're called to board the ferry. Many people try to beat the crowds by arriving early, but if anything your chances of a short wait may be better in the afternoon. As a result of heightened security measures, no bags of any kind are permitted on the ferry.

The center has long been scheduled to hold a new

The attack on Pearl Harbor

As the winter of **1941** approached, with German soldiers occupying most of Europe, and Japanese forces advancing through Southeast Asia, the United States remained outside the global conflict. However, negotiations to halt Japanese progress had stalled, and on November 27 the US government sent secret "war warnings" to its military units: "Japanese future action unpredictable but **hostile action** possible at any moment. If hostilities cannot, repeat cannot, be avoided the United States desires that Japan commit the first overt act."

A few days earlier, a Japanese attack fleet, with six aircraft carriers among its 33 vessels, had sailed from northern Japan. By maintaining strict radio silence, it dodged American surveillance, and sailed for Hawaii along an icy, rarely used northerly course, keeping well clear of usual shipping lanes. The Japanese did not expect to achieve complete surprise, but reconnaissance flights from Pearl Harbor failed to detect their approach. By the early morning of December 7, the fleet was in position 230 miles northwest of Oahu.

The first wave of the attack, consisting of 183 aircraft, was launched at 6am. By 7.53am, the cloud cover had lifted to give the attackers a perfect view of Pearl Harbor, where seven of the US fleet's nine battleships lay at anchor. Within two hours the US Navy lost eighteen warships: eight battleships, three light cruisers, three destroyers and four auxiliary craft. In total, 2403 US military personnel were killed, and 1178 wounded. The Japanese lost 29 aircraft, plus five midget submarines. The next day, declaring the United States to be at war with Japan, President Franklin D. Roosevelt condemned the "dastardly" Pearl Harbor attack as "a date which will live in infamy."

In the long run, the Japanese decision to provoke the US into all-out war in the Pacific was to prove suicidal. What's more, most of the vessels damaged and even sunk at Pearl Harbor eventually returned to active service. Only the *Arizona* and the *Utah* could not be salvaged, while the *Oklahoma* sank once again, 500 miles off the Big Island. By contrast, just two of the Japanese ships that were involved in the attack survived the war; four of the anti-aircraft carriers were sunk during the Battle of Midway. In 1945, the *West Virginia*, risen from the waters of Pearl Harbor, was in Tokyo Bay to witness the Japanese surrender.

museum, designed to trace the events leading up to the attack, the bombing itself, and the course of the war in the Pacific. Only a few exhibits are currently in place, however, including models of both the *Arizona* and the Japanese flagship, the *IMS Akagi* ("Red Castle"). The best place to get a sense of what happened is in the waterfront **garden** outside. From here, you see the low and undramatic mountain ridges that ring Pearl Harbor, together with the gap down the center of the island through which the first planes arrived. Captioned photographs clearly illustrate the disposition of the ships moored along "Battleship Row" on the fateful morning, as well as their eventual fate. Survivors of the attack are often on hand to tell their stories.

When your number finally comes up, you're shown a twenty-minute film, then ushered by Navy personnel onto open-sided boats, which they steer for ten minutes across a tiny fraction of the naval base. You disembark at the memorial, whose white marble walls are inscribed with the names of the dead. The outline of the *Arizona*

▲ USS ARIZONA MEMORIAL

is still discernible in the clear blue waters, and still seeping oil, while here and there rusty metal spurs poke from the water. All those who died when the *Arizona* went down remain entombed in the wreckage, occasionally joined by veteran survivors who choose to be buried here. You're free to stay for as long as you choose, although almost everyone simply returns on the next boat, which usually arrives in around fifteen minutes.

USS Bowfin Submarine Museum and Park

11 Arizona Memorial Drive. Daily 8am–5pm; sub and museum, adults $10, under-13s $4; museum only, adults $5, under-13s $3; combined with *Missouri* admission adults $21, ages 4–12 $11, tickets sold until 2.30pm; ☏808/423-1341, ⊛www .bowfin.org. Located alongside the *Arizona* visitor center, but entirely separate from the national park, the USS Bowfin Submarine Museum and Park serves as an alternative distraction if you have a couple of hours to wait before your ferry. Its main focus, the

claustrophobic *Bowfin* itself, is a still-floating, 83-man submarine that survived World War II unscathed, having sunk 44 enemy vessels. Once you've explored it on a self-guided audio tour – complete with a first-person account of one of the *Bowfin*'s most hair-raising missions, narrated by the captain in charge – you can learn more about the whole story of twentieth-century submarines in the adjoining museum.

The park outside, to which access is free, holds various

▼ USS BOWFIN SUBMARINE MUSEUM

missiles and torpedoes, including a Polaris A-1 ballistic missile, and the Japanese naval equivalent of a kamikaze airplane, a *kaiten*. Such manned, single-seater torpedoes were designed for suicide attacks on larger ships; only one, piloted by its inventor, ever succeeded in sinking a US Navy ship. A memorial garden alongside commemorates 52 US submarines lost during the war in the Pacific, listing over 3500 crew "On Eternal Patrol."

USS Missouri

Ford Island. Daily 8.30am–5pm, tickets sold 8am–3.45pm; adults $16, ages 4–12 $8; Chief's Guided Tours adults $23, ages 4–12 $15; Explorer's Tour adults $40, ages 4–12 $20; ☎ 808/973-2494 or 1-877/644-4489, ⓦ www.ussmissouri.org. Since 1998, the decommissioned battleship *USS Missouri*, also known as the "Mighty Mo," has been permanently moored close to the USS Arizona Memorial. The last battleship to be constructed by the United States, she was christened in January 1944. After service in the Pacific and Korean wars, she was decommissioned in 1955 and remained mothballed until being refitted in 1986. Operation Desert Storm saw the *Missouri* firing Tomahawk missiles against Iraq, but she was finally retired once more in 1992, as the last operational battleship in the world. Should the need arise, she's still capable of being recommissioned in 45–90 days.

Several different US locations competed for the honor of providing a final berth for the *Missouri*. Pearl Harbor won, on the basis that the place where World War II began for the United States should also hold the spot where it ended; the Japanese surrender of September 2, 1945, was signed on the deck

▲ USS MISSOURI

of the *Missouri*, then moored in Tokyo Bay. In addition to being a monument in her own right, part of the battleship's new role is as a recruiting tool for the US Navy; it's even possible to arrange kids' sleep-over parties on board.

Since the battleship is located alongside Ford Island, which is officially part of the naval base, visitors can only reach it by shuttle bus, departing from the USS Bowfin visitor center. Having crossed the harbor on a retracting bridge, you're deposited at the entrance gate. Depending on whether you've paid extra to join one of the regular hour-long "Chief's Guided Tours" – which you might as well, given that you're interested enough to have made it this far – you're then shepherded either towards your personal guide or simply left to climb up to the deck.

The overwhelming first impression for all visitors is the *Missouri*'s sheer size; at 887 feet long, she's the length of three football fields and armed with colossal twin gun turrets. By contrast, once you go below decks, the crew's quarters are cramped in the extreme, bringing home the full claustrophobic reality of her long and dangerous missions. The principal highlights are the dimly lit Combat Engagement Center, set up as it was during the Gulf War but now looking very antiquated; the surrender site, on the deck nearby; and the spot where a kamikaze fighter careered into the side of the ship, as captured in a dramatic photo. Only visitors on the $40 Explorer's Tour get to see the fire and engine rooms, three levels below the main deck.

Southeast Oahu

The high crest of the Ko'olau Mountain Range curves away to the east beyond Honolulu, providing Oahu with its elongated southeastern promontory. The built-up coastal strip is squeezed ever more tightly between the hills and the ocean, but not until you reach Koko Head, eight miles out from Waikīkī and eleven from downtown, do you really feel you've left the city behind. That stands close to lovely Hanauma Bay, where the superb snorkeling waters that fill an extinct volcanic caldera lure thousands of day-tripping visitors.

Beyond Koko Head and Hanauma Bay, the shoreline is so magnificent – punctuated by towering volcanoes, sheltered lagoons, and great beaches – that there have been serious proposals to designate the entire area as a state park devoted to eco-tourism, under the Hawaiian name of Ka Iwi.

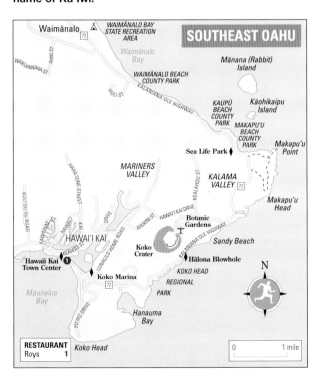

PLACES
Southeast Oahu

Kahāla and Hawaii Kai

The trans-Honolulu "interstate" highway, H-1, ends at the Kahāla Mall, just beyond Diamond Head, to become H-72, or Kalaniana'ole Highway. Both Kahāla itself, and Hawaii Kai further along, are upmarket residential communities that have little to attract visitors, and no desire to encourage them. Hawaii Kai spreads back inland to either side of the large Kuapa Pond, an ancient fishpond that has been remodeled to create the Koko Marina. The main reason to stop is to eat at the dinner-only gourmet restaurant *Roy's*, though the adjoining mall also holds a number of watersports operators. None of the beaches along this stretch merits even a pause

Hanauma Bay Nature Preserve

Daily except Tues: summer 6am–7pm, winter 6am–6pm; open 6am–10pm on 2nd & 4th Sat of each month in summer, and 2nd Sat only in winter. Adults $5, under-13s free, parking $1; arrive by 9am to be sure of a place in the parking lot. ☎808/396-4229. So curved as to be almost round,

beautiful Hanauma Bay, half a mile beyond Hawaii Kai, was created when one side of a volcano collapsed to let in the sea. This spellbinding spot, where a thin strip of palms and sand nestles beneath a green cliff, has long been famous as Oahu's best place to snorkel, and receives almost a million visitors per year. As it's a Marine Life Conservation District, organized tour parties are banned.

A large visitor center overlooks the bay, alongside the stop used by TheBus #22 from Waikīkī. All first-time visitors are required to watch a video here about Hanauma and marine conservation. The beach is five minutes' walk down a gently winding road, and holds showers and drinking fountains but no food or water. A pavilion rents out snorkel equipment, at around $6 per day.

Snorkeling at Hanauma can be a bit like snorkeling in an aquarium. You'll see a lot of fish, but it can all feel rather tame, while the shallowness of the water near the shore can make it hard to stay off the reef.

▼ HANAUMA BAY

Reasonably skilled swimmers who want to see bigger fish can swim out to the deeper waters beyond the inner reef. The largest gap in the reef, at the parking lot end of the bay, is known as the Backdoor Channel, but the current through it can be very strong, and it's safer to use the one known as Telephone Cables, closer to the middle of the beach.

Whether or not you go in the water, it's worth spending a few hours at Hanauma Bay no matter how crowded it is. The crisp green lawns along the foot of the *pali*, dotted with banyan trees, are ideal for picnics.

Koko Head

A dirt road leads away immediately right after the highway turn-off for Hanauma Bay – before the parking lot – to climb straight along the bare ridge above the beach. While the road is closed to drivers, whether it's open to hikers seems to vary. Take it if you can – there are great views from the 642-foot summit of Koko Head, roughly fifteen minutes' walk away. From there you can see back to the similar peak of Diamond Head above Waikīkī, and also walk down a footpath around the lesser of its two craters to peek into the southern end of Hanauma Bay.

Koko Crater

Koko Head Regional Park, which covers Koko Head and Hanauma Bay, extends another couple of miles northeast to take in Koko Crater. The youngest – and thus the largest and most completely formed – of southeastern Oahu's volcanic cones, this is considerably higher than Koko Head and makes a very impressive spectacle. Like its neighbor, it is topped by a double crater. The road up its far side – reached direct from Hawaii Kai, or by doubling back further along the coastal highway – comes to a dead end at Koko Crater Stables. Alongside this you'll find the barely developed Botanic Garden (daily 9am–4pm; free), where a twenty-minute stroll is rewarded by a grove of sweet-smelling, heavy-blossomed plumeria trees. It's not possible to walk up to or around the crater rim, however.

Hālona Blowhole

A couple of miles beyond Hanauma Bay, where Kalaniana'ole Highway squeezes its way between Koko Crater and the ocean, a roadside parking lot enables round-island drivers – and a *lot* of tour buses – to stop off for a look at the Hālona Blowhole. The coastline around here consists of layer upon layer of flat lava, each sheet set slightly back from the one below to form a stairway that climbs up from the sea. At the Hālona Blowhole, the waves have carved out a cave below the visible top layer, and as each new wave rushes in, it's forced out through a small hole to create a waterspout that can reach up to fifty feet high. The blowhole itself does not go straight down, but is stepped; if you fall in – and people do – it's almost impossible to get out.

Little Hālona Cove, to the right of the Blowhole overlook and sheltered by tall stratified cliffs, holds enough sand to make a welcome private beach, if you're lucky enough to have it to yourself. Only swimming within the cove itself is at all safe, and even then only in summer.

Sandy Beach

Avoiding the crowds is not at all
the point at Sandy Beach, half a
mile further on as the shoreline
flattens out between Koko Crater
and Makapu'u Head. Kids from
all over Oahu meet up here most
weekends for what's said to be
the best body-surfing and boogie-
boarding in Hawaii. This is also
one of the few places on the
island where the waves remain
high enough in summer to tempt
pro surfers. Tourists who try to
join in soon find that riding surf
of this size takes a lot of skill and
experience; the beach itself is
notorious for serious injuries. If
you just want to watch, settle
down in the broad sands that lie
southwest of the central lava spit.
There are normally several kite
flyers around as well. Swimming
is never safe at Sandy Beach, but
beyond the spit it's all but
suicidal.

▼ SANDY BEACH

Makapu'u Point

The rising bulk of Oahu's
easternmost point, Makapu'u
Head, pushes Hwy-72 away from
the coastline as it swings round to
run back up the island's
windward flank. Shortly before it
finishes climbing up the last low
incline of the Ko'olau Ridge,
there's just about room to park
beside the road at Makapu'u State
Wayside.

A dirt road here snakes off to
the right, soon curving south
towards the hillock of Pu'u O
Kipahulu. An hour-long hike
(there and back) wends around
the hill and back north along the
line of the coastal cliffs to
Makapu'u Point. From the
railed-off viewing platform at
the end, you can look straight
down the cliffs to the Makapu'u
lighthouse down below, out to
Molokai on the horizon, back to
Koko Head, and up along the
spine of eastern Oahu.

Rounding Makapu'u
Point on the highway –
especially if you manage to
stop at the small official
lookout at the top – is an
equally memorable
experience. The coastal *pali*
suddenly soars away to
your left, while straight
out to sea a couple of tiny
islands stand out in misty
silhouette. The larger of
the two, Manana – also
known as Rabbit Island –
was named for its
population of wild rabbits,
who share their home only
with sea birds.

Makapu'u Beach County Park

Few drivers who skip the
lookout can resist stopping
to drink in the views as
they descend from
Makapu'u Point. The first

▲ MAKAPU'U BEACH

proper parking lot, however, is down below, at Makapuʻu Beach County Park. In summer, this is a broad and attractive strip of sand; in winter, pounded by heavy surf, it's a rocky stretch. Swimming is rarely safe even at the best of times – ask the lifeguards if you're in doubt. Like Sandy Beach (see opposite), however, it's a greatly loved body-surfing and boogie-boarding site, and with the same propensity to lure unwary tourists into the water, it boasts a similarly dismal record of fatalities.

Sea Life Park

Daily 9.30am–5pm; adults $29, ages 4–12 $19; ☎808/259-7933 or 1-866/365-7466, ⊛www .sealifeparkhawaii.com. Immediately opposite the Makapuʻu Beach parking lot is the entrance to the expensive Sea Life Park, which tends to hold greater appeal for children than for their parents. Along with the predictable dolphin and porpoise shows, it holds a giant Reef Tank, a penguin enclosure, and a hospital for injured monk seals. You can also have your own close-up encounter with the dolphins, for a fee that ranges from $99 to $199 for adults, and $69 to $199 for kids, depending on quite how much contact you have. In

addition, the park raises rare green sea turtles for release into the ocean and has even bred a wholphin – half-whale, half-dolphin. A couple of snack bars, where live entertainment is provided by costumed characters, plus a bar run by the Gordon Biersch Brewery, make it all too possible to find yourself spending an entire day here.

Waimānalo

Waimānalo, four miles on from Makapuʻu, holds one of the highest proportions of native Hawaiians of any town on Oahu, and has become a stronghold of supporters of the movement for Hawaiian sovereignty, thanks in part to its role as the home of the late singing superstar Israel Kamakawiwoʻole (see box on p.126). The main drag, lined with fast-food joints, is far from picturesque, but as long as you take care not to intrude, you can get a real glimpse of old-time Hawaii by exploring the backroads. The small family-run farms and nurseries along Waikupanaha Street, which runs inland along the base of the *pali*, are particularly rural and verdant.

The most compelling reason to come to Waimānalo, however, is its beach. At over three miles long, it's the longest stretch of sand on Oahu, and the setting,

PLACES

Southeast Oahu

▲ WAIMĀNALO BEACH

tempted to stroll a long way over the seemingly endless sands.

About a mile further north, where the fir trees backing the beach grow thicker again beyond a residential district, you come to the Waimānalo Bay State Recreation Area. The waves here are a little rougher than those at the county park, but it feels even more secluded, and you can camp for up to five days with a permit from the state parks office in Honolulu ($5; closed Wed & Thurs; see box, p.174).

with high promontories at both ends and a green cradle of cliffs behind, is superb. The most accessible place to park, and also the safest swimming spot, is Waimānalo Beach County Park at its southern end, but wherever you start you're likely to feel

Further on still, and reached by a separate road off the highway, lies Bellows Field Beach Park. Access to this pristine spot, ideal for lazy swimmers and novice

Hawaiian music's biggest star

In 1997, the Hawaiian music scene lost the man who was in every sense its biggest star. **Israel Kamakawiwo'ole**, who was born in Waimānalo in 1959, started out singing in the Makaha Sons of Niihau, and then went solo in 1990, died of respiratory difficulties in a Honolulu hospital. During his twenty-year career, "Iz" came to epitomize the pride and the power of Hawaiian music. His extraordinary voice adapted equally well to rousing political anthems, delicate love songs, pop standards and Jawaiian reggae rhythms, while his personality and his love for Hawaii always shone through both in concert and on record. Like his brother Skippy before him – also a founder member of the Makaha Sons – Iz eventually succumbed to the health problems caused by his immense size. At one point, his weight reached a colossal 757 pounds; he needed a fork-lift truck to get on stage, and could only breathe through tubes. His strength in adversity did much to ensure that he was repeatedly voted Hawaii's most popular entertainer, and after his death he was granted a state funeral, with his body lying in state in the Capitol. His enduring legacy will be the music on his four solo albums – *Ka Ano'i* (1990), *Facing Future* (1993), *E Ala Ē* (1995), and *'n Dis Life* (1996). His medley of "Somewhere Over The Rainbow/What A Wonderful World" is now a staple of movie and TV soundtracks, while his haunting rendition of "Hawai'i 78" (on *Facing Future*) became the anthem of campaigners seeking to restore native Hawaiian sovereignty.

body-surfers, is controlled by the adjoining Air Force base; the public is only allowed in between noon on Friday and 8am on Monday. The county parks office (see box, p.174) runs the campground, which is also open on weekends only.

Restaurants

Roy's

#110, Hawaii Kai Corporate Plaza, 6600 Kalaniana'ole Highway, Hawaii Kai ☎ 808/396-7697, ⓦ www .roysrestaurants.com. Mon–Thurs 5.30–9.30pm, Fri 5.30–10pm, Sat 5–10pm, Sun 5–9.30pm. Gourmet Pacific Rim restaurant, just yards from the sea alongside Hwy-72 ten miles east of Waikīkī, which opened in 1988 as chef Roy Yamaguchi's first Hawaiian venture. His innovative cuisine swiftly became the benchmark for all the top restaurants in Hawaii, and Roy himself has opened branches throughout the state. While renowned as one of Oahu's finest restaurants, it attracts far more locals than tourists; getting here is simply too much of an effort for most Waikīkī-based visitors. It's a noisy, hectic place, where diners can choose between watching the goings-on in the open kitchen or enjoying the views out over Maunalua Bay. The food is consistently excellent, with $8–15 appetizers including individual pizzas, crab cakes, and blackened *ahi*, and $16–30 entrees ranging from garlic-mustard short ribs to the *hibachi*-style salmon selected by President Clinton when he dropped by.

Windward Oahu

Less than ten miles separate downtown Honolulu from Oahu's spectacular windward coast. Climb inland from the city, and at the knife-edge crest of the Ko'olau Mountains you're confronted by amazing views of the serrated *pali* (cliff) that sweeps from northwest to southeast. The beaches below, near the residential communities of Kailua and Kāne'ohe – and Kailua Beach County Park in particular – are glorious.

However, if you're trying to see as much of Oahu as possible on a single day's driving tour, you'd probably do better to avoid Kailua and Kāne'ohe altogether, and head straight off north on H-83. This clings to the coastline all the way up to Oahu's northernmost tip, which is sandwiched between a tempting fringe of golden sand and a ravishing belt of well-watered farmland and tree-covered slopes. On most Hawaiian islands, the windward shore is too exposed to be safe for swimming, but here a protective coral reef makes bathing possible at a succession of narrow, little-used beaches. All are open to the public, but use proper paths to reach them.

Kailua

The shorefront town of Kailua stretches along Kailua Bay roughly four miles down from the Nu'uanu Pali Lookout (see p.112), and four miles north from Waimānolo. Now little more than an exclusive suburb of Honolulu, it was once a favorite dwelling place for the chiefs of Oahu, surrounded by wetlands and rich soil ideal for growing *taro*. Exploring the little side streets that lead off

▼ FRUIT STAND

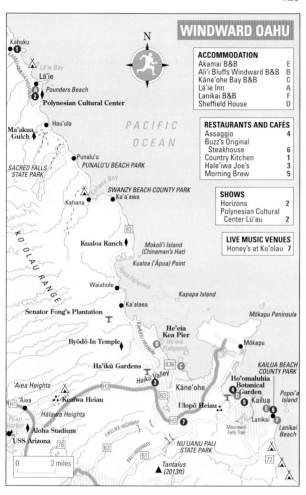

Kalaheo Avenue as it follows the bay may fuel your fantasies of relocating to Hawaii, but inquiring about real estate prices will bring you back to reality, and any time you have here is best spent on the stunning beach. In fact, if quality beach time is your major vacation priority, it's well worth coming to Kailua for the whole day, or even basing

yourself in one of the handful of local B&Bs rather than in Waikīkī.

Almost the only remaining vestige of Kailua's past is Ulupō Heiau, an ancient temple whose construction was attributed to the legendary *menehune* and which later became a *luakini*, dedicated to human sacrifice. This long, low platform of rounded lava boulders looks out

▲ KAILUA BEACH

across the Kawainui Marsh from
a hillock just to the left of Kailua
Road. To get there, take Uluoʻa
Road, the first left turn after
Kailua Road breaks away from
Kalanianaʻole Highway, and then
turn right.

Maunawili Falls Trail

The best way to get out of your
car and into the spectacular
rainforest around Kailua is to
take a half-day hike along the

▼ MAUNAWILI FALLS TRAIL

Maunawili Falls Trail. To reach
the trailhead, follow the Pali
Hwy down from Honolulu.
Opposite the point where
Kamehameha Hwy branches to
the left, you'll see a right turn
onto Auloa Road; don't take it,
but keep going down the Pali
Hwy to the *next* intersection on
the right, which confusingly is
also called Auloa Road. Follow
that, forking left soon to join
Maunawili Road. You'll find the
trailhead just over a mile along,
close to the junction with
Kelewina Road. The trail itself
starts on an unpaved road, but
soon becomes a muddy footpath
through the lush vegetation that
lines the Maunawili Stream.
After about ten minutes, you'll
have to ford the broad stream
for the first of four times; you
may be able to use stepping
stones each time, but don't
depend on it. It's a lovely hike
in itself, with plentiful views of
the wild hills all around, with
the reward at the far end, an
hour or so from the road, of
the low, wide and pretty
Maunawili Falls. The water
beneath the pools is usually
shallow enough to wade right
beneath the flow, but don't try
to climb the slippery stream bed
to the top.

Kailua Beach

Kailua Beach County Park, which fills the colossal main curve of Kailua Bay, is utterly gorgeous – it's the prettiest beach on the whole island – and makes an ideal family swimming spot year-round. The soft wide sands slope down into turquoise waters much used by windsurfers; it's normally possible to rent windsurfing equipment, as well as kayaks, from vans and stalls along the park approach road or on the beach itself. You can also arrange kayak rental by calling Hawaiian Watersports (☎808/255-4352) or Kailua Sailboards and Kayaks (☎808/262-2555). Just be sure to keep away from the area around the Ka'elepulu Canal, which is often turned into a lagoon by a sandbar across its mouth, and can be unpleasantly polluted.

Head north from here, and once past the park you're on Kailua Beach, where the waves hit a little harder, so there's less sand, but swimming conditions are generally safe.

Lanikai

Walking south from the county park beyond Alāla Point brings you within a few hundred yards to the less crowded Lanikai Beach, which is very similar to the park.

Lanikai itself consists of just a few short streets of priceless homes, all but cut off from the rest of Kailua by Ka'iwa Ridge. The coastal road beyond the beach park becomes a one-way loop immediately south of the ridge, forcing you to turn slightly inland on A'alapapa Road. Take the second right here (Ka'elepulu Street), park near the gate of the Mid-Pacific Country Club, and you'll see the Ka'iwa Ridge Trail leading away to the left. Just a few minutes' steep climbing is rewarded with superb views up and down the coast and out to the tiny islands in the bay.

The Mōkapu Peninsula

Kailua's northern limit is defined by Oneawa Ridge, stretching towards the ocean and culminating in the Mōkapu Peninsula. More of an island than a peninsula, joined to the rest of Oahu by two slender causeways, Mōkapu is entirely taken up by a Marine base, and no public access is permitted.

▼ KAYAKING AT KAILUA BEACH

PLACES · Windward Oahu

The newest trans-Koʻolau highway, H-3, was originally commissioned to connect the base with Pearl Harbor. Incidentally, archeologists have found the extensive sand dunes along Mōkapu's northern shore to be the richest ancient burial site in all Hawaii.

Kāneʻohe

Slightly smaller than Kailua, and boasting a far less robust economy, as well as considerably fewer amenities for visitors, Kāneʻohe is seldom seen as an exciting destination in its own right. That's largely because none of its silty beaches are suitable for swimming. However, the seven-mile Kāneʻohe Bay, reaching northwards from the Mōkapu Peninsula, is the largest bay in Hawaii and, once you're outside the main built-up strip, one of the most beautiful. If you want to join the local pleasure-boaters out on the calm waters of the bay, take a one-hour cruise from Heʻeia Kea Pier on the glass-bottomed *Coral Queen* (Mon–Sat 10am, 11am, noon & 1.30pm; adults $15, under-13s $7; ☎808/292-8470).

Heʻeia State Park, on the headland immediately before the pier, is a landscaped area set aside largely for its views of the adjoining Heʻeia Fishpond. Ancient Hawaiians built the low curving stone walls that enclose this saltwater lagoon, which is once again being used to raise mullet. What little you see from the park probably won't hold your attention long, however. Tiny Coconut Island, out to sea, is used for marine research by the University of Hawaii, but is still better known to many thanks to the credits sequence of *Gilligan's Island*.

The Gardens of Kāneʻohe

The quietest and most relaxing of several attractive public gardens that lie inland of Kāneʻohe is the nature reserve of Hoʻomaluhia Botanical Garden (daily 9am–4pm; free), at the top of Luluku Road, which loops back into the hills off Kamehameha Highway between Pali and Likelike highways. Take any of the pleasant short trails away from the visitor center, and you'll soon be out in the wilderness.

If you'd prefer a more commercial display of flowers,

▼ BYŌDŌ-IN TEMPLE

fruits, and orchids, head instead for Senator Fong's Plantation, near Kahalu'u in northern Kāne'ohe (daily 10am–2pm; adults $14.50, under-13s $9; ⊤808/239-6775, ⓦwww .fonggarden.com), where trams whisk visitors along the paved walkways.

The smaller, free Ha'ikū Gardens, just off H-83 at the entrance to glorious Ha'ikū Valley, is an attractive little lily pond that serves mainly to lure diners into the on-site, dinner-only *Hale'iwa Joe's* restaurant (see p.139).

Byōdō-In Temple

Kahekili Hwy, Kāne'ohe. Daily 8.30am–4.30pm; adults $2, under-12s $1. A clearly marked side road *mauka* of H-83 (Kahekili Hwy) just beyond central Kāne'ohe leads to the interdenominational cemetery known as the Valley of the Temples. Several religions have chapels and monuments here, but the one that draws in casual visitors is the Japanese Buddhist Byōdō-In Temple, built in the 1960s to celebrate a hundred years of Japanese immigration to Hawaii. This unexpected replica of a nine hundred-year-old temple at Uji in Japan looks absolutely stunning, its red roofs standing out from the trees at the base of the awesome *pali*.

Having parked outside the temple gates, you cross an arching footbridge to stroll through the peaceful gardens. A fishpond here is so full of orange, gold, and mottled carp that they squeeze each other out of the water in their frenzy for fish food. Before you reach the main pavilion, you're encouraged to ring a three-ton brass bell; you'll probably have heard it echoing through the valley as you arrive.

Once inside (with your shoes left at the threshold), you're confronted by a nine-foot meditating Buddha made of gilded, lacquered wood.

Japanese visitors pay quiet tribute, while excited tourist groups take quick photos of themselves with the Buddha before dashing back to the bus; it's worth sitting for a while before you leave, allowing the tranquility of the place truly to touch you.

Kualoa Point and Mokoli'i

At Ka'alaea, a mile north of the Byōdō-In Temple, Kahekili Highway joins Kamehameha Highway on its way up from He'eia State Park, and the two then run on together as Kamehameha Highway. The tumbling waterfalls at the heads of Waihe'e and Waiahole valleys, visible as you look inland, are superb, but the next point worthy of a halt is at the northern tip of Kāne'ohe Bay.

▼ MOKOLI'I ISLAND

From the crisp green lawns of Kualoa Point, out on the headland, you can look through a straggle of windswept coconut palms to conical Mokoli'i Island. To ancient Hawaiians, this picturesque little outcrop was the tail of a dragon; its more banal modern nickname is "Chinaman's Hat." At low tide, you can wade out to it along the reef – the water should never rise more than waist high, and reef shoes are an absolute must – to find a tiny hidden beach on its northern side. Otherwise, content yourself with a swim back at the point from the thin shelf of sand at Kualoa Park.

Kualoa Ranch

Kamehameha Hwy. 1hr horse or ATV ride $57; 2hr $91; all-day ticket for 4 activities $139. Rates and schedules for specific activities on ☏808/237-7321 or ⓦwww.kualoa.com. Roughly 200 yards north of Kualoa Park, a driveway *mauka* of the highway (left if you're heading north) leads into the expansive grounds of Kualoa Ranch. Until recently a conventional cattle ranch, this now plays host to flocks of Japanese tour groups instead. Individual travelers are welcome to sign up for any of the wide range of activities on offer, which include horse riding, kayaking, a gun range, and all-terrain vehicle excursions, but the place is dominated by large groups of honeymooners.

Ka'a'awa

Several more good beaches lie immediately north of Kāne'ohe Bay, in the area broadly known as Ka'a'awa. There's no danger of failing to spot them; in places the highway runs within a dozen feet of the ocean. So long as the surf isn't obviously high, it's generally safe to park by the road at any of the consecutive Kanenelu, Kalae'ō'io, and Ka'a'awa beaches, and head straight into the water. Only Swanzy Beach County Park, a little further along, really demands caution, on account of its unpredictable currents. It became a beach park thanks to a rich Kailua resident of the 1920s, who donated this land to the state on condition that they didn't create any other public parks nearer her home.

Kahana Valley

Visitor center Mon–Fri 7.30am–4pm; free; ☏808/237-7766. The whole of the deeply indented Kahana Valley, tucked in behind a high serrated *pali* immediately around the corner from the rock formation known as the Crouching Lion, is officially known as Ahupua'a O Kahana

▼ KAHANA BEACH

▲ KAHANA

State Park. Still farmed by native Hawaiian families, it aims to be a "living park;" the residents still grow traditional crops, but don't dress up or pretend to *be* ancient Hawaiians. The beach at Kahana Bay, straight across from the park entrance, hangs onto an ample spread of fine sand all year round, and is very safe for swimming. It's possible to camp in the woods that line its central section; $5 permits are issued by the park visitor center, or the state parks office in Honolulu (see box, p.174).

The easiest of Kahana Valley's attractive (if often rainy) hiking trails, the Kapa'ele'ele Ko'a Trail, ascends the northern flank of the bay for great ocean views. It starts by following the dirt road that heads to the right in front of the visitor center. After passing a few houses, it heads out into a lush meadow scattered with fruit trees, and then veers left at a far from obvious junction to climb into the woods. It soon reaches a clearing where you can gaze across the valley to the high walls on the far side, and watch as it recedes away inland. Not far beyond, a few weather-worn stones mark the site of the

Kapa'ele'ele Ko'a itself, an ancient fishing shrine. A steep climb then leads up to Keaniani Kilo, a *kilo* being a vantage point from which keen-eyed Hawaiians would watch for schools of fish, and signal canoes waiting below to set off in pursuit. There's nothing here now, and young trees have partially obscured the beach, but it's a lovely spot. The trail then drops down to the highway, and you can make your way back along the beach.

The parking lot for the Nakoa Trail, which heads for the back of the valley, is half a mile inland from the visitor center. Assuming that it hasn't been raining (in which case the valley streams will be too high to cross; check at the visitor center), you can then keep walking along the main valley road for another fifteen minutes, before the trail sets off to ramble its way up and around the valley walls. It runs for roughly four miles, with some great views and plenty of mosquitoes to keep you company. For a shorter adventure, simply head left at the very start and you'll soon come to an idyllic little swimming hole in Kahana Stream.

Hau'ula and Punalu'u

Beyond Kahana Valley, the highway continues to cling to every curve of the coastline, and traffic tends to move slowly. Island maps show Hau'ula and Punalu'u as being distinct towns, but on the ground it's hard to tell where one ends and the next begins. Both are quiet little local communities that barely reach a hundred yards back from the shore.

Of the half-dozen named beaches in this stretch, Punalu'u Beach Park, the furthest south, is the best for swimming, so long as you keep away from the mouth of Wai'ono Stream. The strip of sand is so thin at this point that the coconut palms rooted in the lawns behind it manage to curve out over the waves. Hau'ula Beach Park, a few miles along, is equally sheltered, but only snorkelers derive much pleasure from swimming out over the rocks.

Hau'ula trails

Three exhilarating but muddy trails enable hikers to explore Ma'akua Gulch, behind central

▼ HAU'ULA VALLEY

Hau'ula. To reach them, continue *mauka* (inland) along Ma'akua Road from the end of the straight stretch of Hau'ula Homestead Road that starts opposite the northern limit of Hau'ula Beach Park. (Hau'ula Homestead Road actually loops round to meet Kamehameha Highway at two separate points; it's the northern section that you need to find.) The entrance gate to the trail network is a hundred yards up Ma'akua Road, alongside a small parking lot.

The best short hike is the Hau'ula Loop Trail, which branches off to the right from just beyond the gate. In something under two hours, with a few stretches of steep climbing, it carries you up and over the high ridge to the north, through sweet-smelling forests of ironwood and pine. As well as views across the ocean, you get amazing panoramas of neighboring Kaipapa'u Valley, reaching far inland and looking as though no human has ever entered it.

The similar but more overgrown Ma'akua Ridge Trail twists its own circuit around the southern wall of the gulch, while the Ma'akua Gulch Trail follows the central stream back towards the mountains. As the gulch narrows, you're forced to hike more and more in the stream bed itself, making this a very dangerous route after rain. Otherwise, it's a good opportunity to see the luscious blossoms for which Hau'ula – meaning "red *hau* trees" – is named.

Lā'ie

The neat, even prim air of the town of Lā'ie, three miles on from Hau'ula, is understandable once you learn that it was founded by Mormons in 1864, and remains dominated by the Latter-day Saints to this day. This was the second major Mormon settlement in Hawaii; the first, on Lanai, was abandoned when church elders discovered that its president, William Gibson, had registered all its lands in his own name. Gibson went on to be prime minister of Hawaii, while his congregation moved to Oahu. Lā'ie now holds an imposing Mormon Temple, built in 1919 as the first such temple outside the continental United States (a visitor center, not the temple itself, is open daily 9am–9pm), and a branch of the Mormon-run Brigham Young University, but is best known to visitors for a less obviously Mormon enterprise, the Polynesian Cultural Center.

Mormon colleges tend not to spawn lively alternative scenes, and Lā'ie is no exception. Local students do at least get to body-surf the heavy waves at Pounders Beach at the south end of town, but if you lack their know-how don't be tempted to join in. Kokololio Beach just south of that is an attractive curve of sand where swimming is only safe in summer, while Lā'ie Beach in the center of town is prone to strong currents. The two-part Mālaekahana Bay State Recreation Area further north provides the best local recreational swimming, and also makes an excellent place to camp (pick up a free state permit in Honolulu; see box, p.174). At low tide, it's possible to wade out from here to Goat Island, a bird sanctuary where the Mormons once kept their goats, which has a beautiful protected beach on its north shore.

▲ LŪ'AU PERFORMERS AT THE CULTURAL CENTER

The Polynesian Cultural Center

An incredible one million paying customers each year head to Lā'ie for the **Polynesian Cultural Center**. Billed as a "cultural theme park," it's a large, landscaped compound where each of seven separate "villages" is dedicated to a different island group. In addition to Hawaii, Tahiti, and the Marquesas, the further-flung cultures of Fiji, Tonga, Samoa, and New Zealand are represented. Rather than reconstructing an actual place, each village includes a few typical structures, with indoor and outdoor space for demonstrations of traditional crafts and activities, ranging from food production or wood carving to music, dances, fire-walking, and games. As an introduction to the enormous diversity of the Pacific, it's not at all bad, though the emphasis is very much on entertainment, and kids are likely to enjoy it more than adults.

Unless you time your visit to each village to coincide with the intricate daily schedule of presentations, there's not much to see, so if you're going to come at all be prepared to spend at least half a day in total. As well as touring the villages, you can also ride up and down the central lagoon in a large canoe, or take a tram trip into Lā'ie. The compound also holds an IMAX cinema, free to all visitors, and countless souvenir and gift stores, snack bars, and restaurants. All remain open into the evening, but the main reason visitors stay on after the villages close up, at around 5.30pm, are the two shows – the *lū'au* and *Horizons*, described on p.140.

The Polynesian Cultural Center is largely staffed by students from the adjoining university – who don't necessarily come from the relevant parts of the Pacific – and subsidizes programs and scholarships there. Bear in mind that the information it presents is laced with Mormon theology,

and can thus be wildly divergent from conventional cultural and academic beliefs.

Kahuku

Kahuku, a couple of miles on from Lā'ie, may look run-down by comparison, but is considerably more atmospheric. Though the plantation it served went out of business in 1971, the rusting hulk of the Kahuku Sugar Mill still overshadows this small town. Assorted outbuildings now house a half-hearted shopping mall, but it's all in a sorry state. Unidentified lumps of machinery are dotted around the courtyard, painted in peeling pastel blues and yellows. Most of the old mill workings remain in place, though, with some parts color-coded according to their former function. Nearby, you can also pick up freshly cooked shrimp from a couple of white trucks

Visiting the Polynesian Cultural Center

Quite simply, there's no cheap way to visit the **Polynesian Cultural Center** (Mon–Sat noon–9pm). Each of its various "packages" entitles you to explore the seven villages, take a canoe ride and tram tour, and see an Imax movie. The Admission/Show Package (adult $55, ages 3–11 $40) also offers seating at the *Horizons* show. All the more expensive packages include some sort of meal, but there are fast-food options available on site if you'd rather not pay extra. With the Ali'i Lū'au Package ($80/$56) you get a flower *lei*, a ticket for the *lū'au*, and better seating at the show; the Ambassador Package ($115/$80) gives you a guided tour, a fancier *lei*, an "Ambassador Buffet" dinner instead of the *lū'au*, even better seating at the show, and various other fripperies; the Ambassador Lū'au Package ($115/$80) is the same but you go to the *lū'au* instead of the buffet; and the Super Ambassador Package ($205/$155) buys "fine dining" rather than the *lū'au*, plus loads of extra behind-the-scenes tours. With each of those packages, you can return to the center within the next three days to explore any villages you've missed, but the only show you're entitled to see is the IMAX film. In addition, each package offers a Twilight version, in which you can arrive at the center at 4pm or later and pay a reduced rate of around $10–20 below the usual fee, this time with no re-admission privileges.

Finally, the center also offers round-trip transportation from Waikīkī, at $19 per person (no reductions) for a seat in a motorcoach, or $28 for a mini-bus. It costs $5 to park your own vehicle at the center.

For all reservations, contact ☎808/293-3333 or 1-800/367-7060, ⓦwww.polynesia.com.

stationed permanently beside the highway; of the two, *Giovanni's*, to the south, serves the spicier food.

Behind the sugar mill are a few dirt lanes holding tin-roofed plantation homes. The long beach beyond is not suitable for swimming, but stretches a full five miles up to Turtle Bay, should you fancy a solitary, bracing hike.

Beyond Kahuku, the highway veers away from the shore to run alongside the Amorient Aquafarms. Fresh shrimp from this series of ponds can be bought from trucks and vans stationed along the highway nearby. The Walsh Farms complex of small, brightly painted shacks and funky vans at the far end sells fresh fruit, shrimp, and an entertaining mixture of antiques and junk.

Shops

Book Ends

600 Kailua Rd, Kailua ☎808/261-1996. Mon–Sat 9am–8pm, Sun 9am–5pm. The archetypal small community bookstore, where you're welcome to sit and chat for a while or simply browse the eclectic selection of new and used books, with a big Hawaiiana section as well as every imaginable kind of fiction and non-fiction.

Cafés

Morning Brew

572 Kailua Rd, Kailua ☎808/262-7770. Daily 6am–8pm. Friendly local coffee bar in central Kailua, with a full range of coffee drinks, pastries, healthy sandwiches, and salads, that's bravely clinging on despite the presence of *Starbuck's* opposite.

Restaurants

Assaggio

354 Uluniu Rd, Kailua ☎808/261-2772. Mon–Thurs 11.30am–2.30pm & 5–9.30pm, Fri & Sat 11.30am–2.30pm & 5–10pm, Sun 5–9.30pm. Wildly popular upmarket Italian restaurant that's always busy, despite being hidden on a quiet side street a block north of central Kailua. As well as dozens of pasta dishes for under $15, like fettucini Alfredo and eggplant parmigiani, they offer nine styles of chicken, including stuffed with ricotta cheese for $15, and fish of the day cooked as you choose for around $20.

Buzz's Original Steakhouse

413 Kawailoa Rd, Kailua ☎808/261-4661. Daily 11am–3pm & 5–10pm. Though the food – wood-grilled steaks, fresh fish, salad bar, and cocktails – is nothing amazing, *Buzz's* location, opposite Kailua Bay, is ideal when you're feeling too lazy to stray from the beach. Set among the palms, with a wraparound *lāna'i* and cooling water sprinklers, it has a distinctly island feel that's difficult to resist.

Country Kitchen

Kahuku Sugar Mill, 56-565 Kamehameha Hwy, Kahuku ☎808/293-2110. Mon–Sat 9am–5pm. Simple, welcoming local diner that serves up cooked breakfasts plus shrimp and barbecue special later on.

Hale'iwa Joe's

Ha'ikū Gardens, Kahekili Hwy, Kāne'ohe ☎808/247-6671. Mon–Thurs 5.30–9.30pm, Fri & Sat 5.30–10.30pm. Another branch in Hale'iwa, see p.150. Dinner-only steak and seafood restaurant, set beside a lily pond in lovely Ha'ikū Valley.

Generally fishy appetizers, like ceviche or sushi, for under $10, with conventional chicken or beef entrees at up to $20.

Live music venues

Honey's at Koʻolau

Koʻolau Golf Club, 45-550 Kionaole Rd, Kāneʻohe ☎808/236-4653. You'll need a car, and a good map, to find this unlikely, and truly wonderful, Windward hangout. Cross the mountains from Honolulu on the Pali Hwy, turn left onto Kamehameha Hwy, and then left again immediately north of H-3; *Honey's* is downstairs in the clubhouse (and the "Honey" in question is Don Ho's mother). The reason to make the effort? Genial ukulele wizard Eddie Kamae, founder member of the Sons of Hawaii, presides over a hugely enjoyable afternoon jam session, often with big-name guests and enjoyed by a lively local crowd, Sun 3.30–6pm. Arrive early to get a good seat; full food menu available. No cover.

Shows

Horizons

Polynesian Cultural Center, Lāʻie. ☎808/293-3333 or 1-800/367-7060, ⓦwww.polynesia.com. Cheapest admission adult $55, ages 3–11 $40; all ticketing options explained in box on p.138. Mon–Sat 7.30pm.

The Polynesian Cultural Center's ninety-minute evening show has been running for almost fifty years. Now held in a high-tech 2800-seat theater, it's a slick, undemanding revue of chants, songs, and dances from six different island groups, performed by a hundred-strong cast. It still includes the Fijian number "Bula Laie," which Elvis Presley filmed here as "Drums Of The Islands" for the 1966 movie *Paradise Hawaiian Style*.

Polynesian Cultural Center Lūʻau

Polynesian Cultural Center, Lāʻie. ☎808/293-3333 or 1-800/367-7060, ⓦwww.polynesia.com. Cheapest admission adult $80, ages 3–11 $56; all ticketing options

▼ *LŪʻAU AT* POLYNESIAN CULTURAL CENTER, WINDWARD OAHU

explained on p.138. Mon–Sat 5.15pm.

Guests file into the *lū'au* theater at the Polynesian Cultural Center to be seated at several tiers of communal tables, facing an open-air stage, where Hawaiian musician and dancers (many of them children) salute the sunset and perform an easy-listening medley of island songs. People from each table in turn are shepherded to the back of the theater to load their plates with an uninspiring buffet dinner. No alcohol is served. All *lū'au* tickets also include admission to the more spectacular *Horizons* show described opposite.

The North Shore

If you have the slightest interest in surfing, even if it's as a spectator rather than a participant, you'll need no persuading to visit Oahu's legendary North Shore. Surfing beaches such as beach parks like Waimea, Sunset, and ʻEhukai are famous the world over, and for their scenic beauty as well as their perfect waves they're in a totally different league from Waikīkī.

However, the area as a whole is surprisingly under-equipped for tourists; even the best-known beaches are much more laid-back than you might expect, and you can usually find a quiet spot to yourself. In summer, the tame waves may leave you wondering what all the fuss is about; see them at full tilt in the winter, between October and April, and you'll have no doubts.

If you plan to do some surfing yourself – and this is no place for amateurs – then you'd do best to base yourself in Pūpūkea (see p.174). Otherwise, you can see all there is to see in an easy day-trip from Waikīkī, with a pause to shop and snack in Haleʻiwa.

Haleʻiwa

The main town on the North Shore stands where Kamehameha Highway reaches the ocean, 24 miles north of Honolulu. For most visitors, Haleʻiwa (pronounced "ha-lay-eve-a") comes as a pleasant surprise. It's one of the very few communities on Oahu whose roots have not

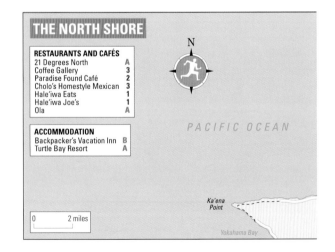

THE NORTH SHORE

RESTAURANTS AND CAFÉS
21 Degrees North	A
Coffee Gallery	3
Paradise Found Café	2
Cholo's Homestyle Mexican	3
Haleʻiwa Eats	1
Haleʻiwa Joe's	1
Ola	A

ACCOMMODATION
Backpacker's Vacation Inn	B
Turtle Bay Resort	A

N

PACIFIC OCEAN

Kaʻena Point

0   2 miles

Yokohama Bay

been obscured by a century of rebuilding and development, despite the fact that tourists have been coming here ever since the opening of a railroad from Honolulu in 1899.

Since the 1960s, the town has become a gathering place for surfers from all over the world. Many of the first arrivals, lured here from California by the cult movie *Endless Summer*, seem to have remained not only in Hawaii, but also in the 1960s. The town these days is still bursting with businesses like surf shops, tie-dye stores, wholefood restaurants, and galleries of ethnic knick-knacks. Add those to a scattering of upfront tourist traps, and local stores and diners, and you've got an intriguing, energetic blend that entices many travelers to stay for months.

▲ SURF MUSEUM, HALE'IWA

That said, there's precious little to see in Hale'iwa. Its main street, Kamehameha Avenue, runs for a mile from the Paukauila Stream to the Anahulu River, well back from the ocean, passing a cluster of gas stations and then a succession of low-rise, funky malls. In the largest of these, the North Shore Marketplace, a storefront proclaiming itself a

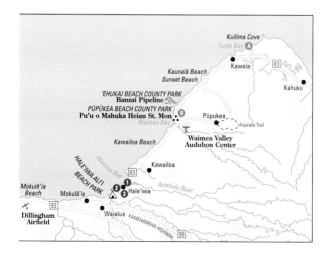

Surf Museum (open "most afternoons"; free) traces the history of Hawaiian surfboards from the hollow wooden boards of the 1930s through early fiberglass models from the 1950s, and holds shrines to Duke Kahanamoku in particular, and the 1960s in general.

Only as you approach the river do you finally come to the heart of Hale'iwa, a short stretch of old-fashioned boardwalk lined with false-front wooden buildings. One of these houses is Matsumoto's, a Japanese grocery store that has become so renowned for its shave ice – the Hawaiian equivalent of a sno-cone, a mush of ice saturated with sickly sweet syrup – that it's now an all-but-obligatory stop on round-island tours.

The beaches of Hale'iwa

At the far end of Hale'iwa, the narrow Rainbow Bridge crosses Anahulu River, affording great views upstream towards the green slopes of the Anahulu Valley. The small bay at the rivermouth is Waialua Bay, with Hale'iwa Harbor sheltered by a breakwater on its southwestern side. Southwest of the harbor, Hale'iwa Ali'i Beach Park is a favorite place for local kids to learn to surf – there are even free surfing lessons on weekend mornings in winter – but inexperienced outsiders who have a go are taking their lives in their hands. That was the pretext for making this the fictional location of the TV show *Baywatch Hawaii*, a short-lived, state-subsidized experiment in relocating the Californian show to Hawaii that cost Hawaiian taxpayers dear.

Just to reach the waves at Hale'iwa Ali'i, you have to pick your way across a tricky shallow coral reef; once you're out there you're at the mercy of strong crosscurrents. You're better off swimming at Hale'iwa Beach Park, on the northeast shore of the bay, where it's much safer.

Waimea Bay

Long Kawailoa Beach stretches for almost five miles northeast of Hale'iwa, interrupted repeatedly by rocky reefs and swept by fierce currents. Driving along the highway, however, virtually the first glimpse you get of the ocean is as you crest a small promontory to look down on Waimea Bay. This is perhaps the most famous surfing spot in the world, thanks to what are generally believed to be the biggest rideable waves on the planet. During the summer, it's often calm as a lake, but in winter the break off its craggy headlands can remain over twenty feet high for days at a time. Anywhere else, even the waves right on the beach would count as monsters, and lethal rip currents tear along the shoreline. While entering the ocean at Waimea in winter is extremely dangerous for anyone other than expert surfers, the beautiful sands of Waimea Bay Beach County Park are usually crowded with swimmers, snorkelers, and boogie-boarders in summer.

Until a huge flood in 1894, Waimea River flowed freely into the sea, and the valley behind was densely populated. Most of its farms and homes were destroyed, however, and the mouth of the river is now blocked by a sandbar that forms part of the beach park.

Waimea Valley Audubon Center

Kamehameha Hwy. Daily 9.30am–5pm; adults $8, ages 4–12 $5; parking $2; ☎808/638-9199, ⓦwww.audubon.org. Inland of the

▲ WAIMEA VALLEY AUDUBON CENTER

highway bridge that crosses Waimea River, one of Oahu's most beautiful valleys is run as the Waimea Valley Audubon Center. While primarily a botanical center showcasing carefully maintained, scrupulously labeled gardens planted with Polynesian flowers and trees, the valley also holds a number of archeological sites. The most prominent, the restored *Hale O Lono* or "House of Lono," is an ancient *heiau* or temple whose three stone terraces rise next to the main gate; in fact you can take a look without paying to enter. Once inside the center proper, you can wander for roughly a mile along stream-side walkways that pass the fenced-off ruins of further *heiaus* and ancient burial sites, as well as a mock-up of a Hawaiian village. Just be sure you wear repellent to deter the ever-present mosquitoes. Following the path to the far end, a lovely walk even if you have no great interest in learning about plants, brings you to the double, sixty-foot Waimea Falls at the head of the valley. Visitors are permitted to swim in the pool below.

Pūpūkea

Immediately beyond Waimea Bay, Kamehameha Highway starts to cruise beside a succession of magnificent surfing beaches. Driving here demands patience; at the best of times, vehicles pull off without warning, while during major competitions traffic slows to a virtual standstill.

Pūpūkea Beach County Park, which, like Hanauma Bay (see p.122), is a Marine Life Conservation District, stretches for well over a mile from the mouth of Waimea Bay. At its western end, the Three Tables surf break is named after three flat-topped chunks of reef, where plenty of unwary swimmers have come to grief, while Shark's Cove to the east, riddled with submarine caves, is a popular site for snorkelers and scuba divers in summer. The low-key community of Pūpūkea itself holds a few stores, but no restaurants.

Pu'u O Mahuka Heiau State Monument

For a superb view of Waimea Valley and the bay, head up to the Pu'u O Mahuka Heiau, perched on the eastern bluff above the mouth of the river. As Oahu's largest temple of human sacrifice, this was once home to a terrifying brotherhood of *pahupu* warrior-priests. To reach it, turn

▼ PU'U O MAHUKA

▲ 'EHUKAI BEACH PARK

off the coastal highway at the Foodland supermarket, a few hundred yards beyond the bay. Having climbed the hill on twisting Pūpūkea Road, turn right onto a narrow paved track that skirts the cliff edge for just under a mile.

The parking lot at the end of the track is alongside the higher of the temple's two tiers. The meadow that appears to lie just beyond the *heiau* is in fact on the far side of the deep cleft of Waimea Valley. Trails lead around and partly through the old stone walls, within which it's easy to make out the outlines of several subsidiary structures; most were originally paved with water-worn stones carried up from Waimea Bay. The main "altar" at the *mauka* end, which is usually covered with offerings of flower *leis*, pineapples, vodka, and water, probably bears little resemblance to its original configuration. From the little loop path around the java plum trees nearby, you can see right along the North Shore to Ka'ena Point in the western distance; the *heiau* was positioned here partly so that beacon fires could signal to Wailua on Kauai.

Kaunala Trail

Beyond the *heiau* turnoff, Pūpūkea Road heads inland for another two miles, to end at the gates of a Boy Scout Camp. From here, the five-mile Kaunala Trail, open to the public on weekends only, runs along the thickly wooded crest of a high mountain ridge. As well as views of the deep and inaccessible gorges to either side, if the clouds clear you'll eventually see Oahu's highest peak, 4020-foot Mount Ka'ala, far across the central plains.

Sunset and 'Ehukai beaches

With its wide shelf of yellow sand, lined by palm trees, Sunset Beach, to the northeast of Pūpūkea, is perhaps the most picture-perfect beach on Oahu. Only occasional gaps between the oceanfront homes allow access, but once you get there you're free to wander for two blissful miles of paradise-island

▼ SURFING AT SUNSET BEACH

▲ KUILIMA COVE AND TURTLE BAY RESORT

coastline. Unless you come on a calm and current-free summer's day (ask the lifeguards), it's essential to stay well away from the water; the "Sunset Rip" has been known to drag even beachcombers out to sea.

In winter, when the waves are stupendous, Sunset Beach fills with photographers in search of the definitive surfing shot, while reckless pro surfers perform magazine-cover stunts out on the water. Each of the breaks here has its own name, the most famous being the Banzai Pipeline, where the goal is to let yourself be fired like a bullet through the tubular break and yet manage to avoid being slammed down onto the shallow, razor-sharp reef at the end. To watch the action, walk a few hundred yards west (left) from 'Ehukai Beach County Park, to where a small patch of lawn separates the beach from the road.

Sunset Beach, a mile past 'Ehukai, was where North Shore surfing first took off, following advances in surfboard technology in the early 1950s, and remains the venue for many contests. The break known as Backyards is renowned for being especially

lethal, though it's a popular playground for windsurfers. Kaunala Beach beyond that, the home of the Velzyland break, is the last major surf spot before the highway curves away towards Turtle Bay (see below) and the Windward Coast. Velzyland offers reliable rather than colossal waves, but riding them with any degree of safety requires immense precision.

Turtle Bay

Just before Kamehameha Highway rejoins the ocean on the North Shore, an obvious spur road leads *makai* past some expensive condos and private homes to end at Turtle Bay. Photogenic beaches lie to either side of Kuilima Point here – long, wave-raked Turtle Bay to the west, and the sheltered artificial lagoon of Kuilima Cove to the east – but apart from surfers the only visitors likely to head this way are those staying at the luxury *Turtle Bay Resort* on the point itself, reviewed on p.174.

If you're traveling by bus, note that the resort marks the spot where TheBus #55 from the south becomes #52 as it heads west, and vice versa.

▲ TURTLE BAY

West from Hale'iwa: Waialua and Mokulē'ia

The coast of northern Oahu to the west of Hale'iwa lacks suitable surfing beaches, and is so rarely visited that most people don't really count it as part of the North Shore at all.

The area's principal landmark is the Waialua Sugar Mill, slowly rusting away at the foot of the Wai'anae mountains since the closure of the local sugar company in 1996. A moderately interesting driving tour leads down the backroads of the village of Waialua and along oceanfront Crozier Drive to even smaller Mokulē'ia, but while that gives you attractive views of Hale'iwa in the distance, you might as well go straight to Hale'iwa itself.

Ka'ena Point

The westernmost promontory of Oahu, Ka'ena Point, is only accessible on foot or mountain bike; it's not possible to drive all the way around from the North Shore to the Leeward Shore. As Farrington Highway runs west of Waialua and Mokulē'ia, the landscape grows progressively

drier, and the road eventually grinds to a halt a couple of miles beyond Dillingham Airfield.

On the far side of the gate where the road finally ends, you can follow either a bumpy, dusty dirt road beside the steadily dwindling Wai'anae Ridge, or a sandy track that straggles up and down across the coastal rocks. The only sign of life is likely to be the odd local fisherman, perched on the spits of black lava reaching into the foaming ocean.

After roughly an hour of hot hiking, the ridge vanishes altogether, and you squeeze between boulders to enter the Ka'ena Point Natural Area Reserve. This largely flat and extremely windswept expanse of gentle sand dunes, knitted together with creeping ivy-like *naupaka*, is used as a nesting site in winter by Laysan albatrosses. At the very tip, down below a rudimentary lighthouse – a slender white pole topped by flashing beacons – tiny little beaches cut into the headland. Winter waves here can reach more than fifty feet high, the highest recorded anywhere in the world, and way beyond the abilities of any surfer, though humpback whales often come in close to the shore.

From Ka'ena Point, you can see the mountains curving away down the leeward coast, as well as the white "golfball" of a military early-warning system up on the hills. Just out to sea is a rock known as Pōhaku O Kaua'i ("the rock of Kauai"); in Hawaiian legend, this is a piece of Kauai, which became stuck to Oahu when the demi-god Maui attempted to haul all the islands together.

outfitter in Hale'iwa; look for the brightly painted van to the left of the highway immediately across Rainbow Bridge. As well as selling new and used boards and souvenirs, they rent surfboards ($6 per hour, $30 per day), body-boards ($5/$20), windsurfing boards ($13/$50), and snorkel equipment ($7 half-day, $10 all day); organize quality dive trips (shore dives one tank $75, two tanks $100; two-tank boat dives $110); and provide lessons in surfing and windsurfing ($75 for two hours, $160 half-day).

Shops

Barnfield's Raging Isle Surf & Cycle

North Shore Marketplace, 66-250 Kamehameha Hwy, Hale'iwa ⏀808/637-7700, ⓦwww.ragingisle .com. Equipment, clothing, shoes, and accessories for surfers and cyclists, with a massive selections of bikes for sale or rent; mountain bikes cost from $40 for 24hr.

Surf 'n' Sea

62-595 Kamehameha Hwy, Hale'iwa ⏀808/637-9887 or 1-800/899-7873, ⓦwww.surfnsea.com. Daily 9am–7pm. The best-known surf

Cafés

Coffee Gallery

North Shore Marketplace, 66-250 Kamehameha Hwy, Hale'iwa ⏀808/637-5355. Daily 6.30am–8pm. Deliciously cool dark-wood gallery where you can sit and drink espresso drinks, funky smoothies and fresh juices; they also serve a small selection of wraps and burritos.

Paradise Found Café

66-443 Kamehameha Hwy, Hale'iwa ⏀808/637-4540. Mon–Sat 9am–5pm, Sun 9am–4pm. Friendly little wholefood café at the west end of

▼ SURF 'N' SEA

Hale'iwa, consisting of a few colorful booths at the back of the Celestial Natural Foods store where you can pick up delicious veggie breakfasts from $6, humungous lunches for $7–10, and thirst-quenching fresh fruit smoothies from $4.

Restaurants

21 Degrees North

Turtle Bay Resort, 57-091 Kamehameha Hwy ☎808/293-8811, ext 6538. Tues–Sat 6–10pm. Signature restaurant at the plush *Turtle Bay Resort*, reached via an impressive, if kitschy, enclosed walkway of waterfalls and palms, is a comfortable and elegant spot, with minimal Eastern accents and huge picture windows. Both its indoor and outdoor seating offer great views of the foaming white North Shore surf, spotlit at night, while the flavorful New Hawaiian menu features appetizers like pan-seared scallops and shrimp satay ($13) and entrees ($28–40) such as pan-seared *moi* wrapped in nori or mac-nut rack of lamb. A five-course prix fixe dinner costs $76, or $95 with specially selected wines.

Cholo's Homestyle Mexican

North Shore Marketplace, 66-250 Kamehameha Hwy, Hale'iwa ☎808/637-3059. Daily 8am–9pm. Festive, very lively Mexican joint with some outdoor seating – complete with scrawny chickens scratching in the dirt. The long menu offers the usual favorites – and a few more local choices, including *ahi* quesadillas – for around $8–12, with plenty of combos at up to $15, and a good range of icy mojitos.

Hale'iwa Eats

66-079 Kamehameha Hwy, Hale'iwa ☎808/637-4247. Daily except Mon noon–8pm. Glass-fronted diner, not far from the ocean in central Hale'iwa, that serves good, simple Thai curries and noodle dishes for under $10.

Hale'iwa Joe's

66-011 Kamehameha Hwy, Hale'iwa ☎808/637-8005. Mon–Thurs & Sun 11.30am–9.30pm, Fri & Sat 11.30am–10.30pm. Conventional, heavily touristed steak house at the mouth of the Anahulu River near Hale'iwa harbor, with an outdoor terrace at the back. At lunchtime, sandwiches or salads cost around $10, and most of the items on the dinner menu are also available; in the evening, sushi or *poke* appetizers cost around $8 and steamed fish more like $20, while a New York steak is $25.

Ola

Turtle Bay Resort, 57-091 Kamehameha Hwy ☎808/293-0801. Mon–Thurs & Sun 11am–3pm & 5.30–9.30pm, Fri & Sat 11am–3pm & 5.30–10pm. Set right on the sands of Kuilima Cove, footsteps away from the ocean and open to the warm breezes, this effortlessly stylish and relaxed place is the perfect island restaurant. The contemporary Hawaiian cuisine is exceptional, based on fresh ingredients and regional specialties – try the slow-poached togarashi smoked salmon with sweet potato and edamame succotash – and the laid-back atmosphere makes it hard to leave.

Central Oahu

Thanks to the island's slender central "waist", much of the quickest route from Honolulu to the North Shore lies across the flat agricultural heartland of central Oahu. Cradled between the mountains, the Leilehua Plateau was created when lava flowing from the Ko'olau eruptions lapped against the older Wai'anae Range. Sugar cane and pineapples raised in its rich volcanic soil were the foundation of the Hawaiian economy until less than fifty years ago. As commercial farming has dwindled, however, the area has acquired a dejected atmosphere. More people than ever live in towns such as Waipahu and Wahiawā – many of them personnel from the military bases tucked into the hillsides – but there's very little here to interest tourists. If you plan to drive around Oahu in a single day, you'd do better to press straight on to Hale'iwa (see p.142).

(see p.142)

'Aiea and Pearl City

Whichever road you follow, you have to drive a long way west of Honolulu before you reach open countryside. H-1, the main "interstate," curves past the airport and Pearl Harbor, while Hwy-78 sticks closer to the Ko'olau foothills, but they eventually crisscross each other to run through the nondescript communities of 'Aiea and Pearl City. Restaurants where commuters can grab a quick meal appear on all sides, but neither town has a center worth stopping for.

Keaīwa Heiau State Park

Open 24hr. Only Keaīwa Heiau State Park, on a hilltop above 'Aiea proper, merits a detour

▼ KEAĪWA HEIAU STATE PARK

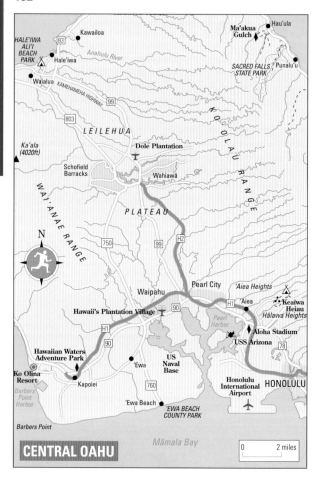

CENTRAL OAHU

	2 miles
0	

from the highway, and even then appeals more to local residents than to outsiders. 'Aiea Heights Drive, the road that leads up to it, heads right from the second stoplight after the Aloha Stadium turnoff on H-78, and then twists for almost three miles through a sleepy residential area.

Keaīwa Heiau, whose ruined walls are on the left as soon as you enter the park, was a center where healers known as *kahuna*

lapa'au once practiced herbal medicine, using plants cultivated in the surrounding gardens. The most famous of those healers was Keaīwa – "the mysterious" – himself. Lots of *ti* plants, together with a few larger *kukui* trees, still grow within the otherwise well-maintained precinct, which also holds a little shrine and a central ring of stones that encloses a small lawn. This layout is largely conjectural, however, as the *heiau* was severely damaged during the sugar plantation era.

There are no views from the *heiau*, but a mile-long loop road circles the ridge that lies beyond, where the ironwood forest is punctuated with meadows and picnic areas looking out over Pearl Harbor. Halfway around, you'll come to the trailhead for the 'Aiea Loop Trail, a five-mile circuit through the woods with views of the interior valleys as well as Honolulu. The highlight is the wreckage of a World War II cargo plane that crashed into a remote gully.

Should you plan to stay, camping at the park's cool, secluded campground (closed Wed and Thurs) costs $5, with a state permit (see p.174).

Waipahu

Just beyond Pearl City, both H-2 and Kamehameha Highway branch away to head north across the central plateau. Only a mile or so west, however, the small town of Waipahu holds one of Hawaii's best historical museums, as described below. It's also home to the unexpectedly upmarket Waikele Center shopping mall, with its giant Borders bookstore and lots of discount "factory outlets."

Hawaii's Plantation Village

94-695 Waipahu, Waipahu. Mon–Fri 9am–3pm, Sat 10am–3pm; Hourly guided tours depart Mon–Sat 10am–2pm; adults $13, seniors $10, under-12s $5; ☎808/677-0110, ⊛www.hawaiiplantationvillage.org. A mile south of H-1 in Waipahu, just below the sugar mill to which it owes its existence, stands Hawaii's Plantation Village. An evocative memorial to the early days of immigration, it's a loving, nonprofit re-creation of the living conditions of the almost 400,000 agricultural laborers who migrated to Hawaii between 1852 and 1946, and were largely responsible for spawning the ethnic blend of the modern state.

Enthusiastic local guides lead visitors around a small museum and then through a "time tunnel" onto the former plantation estate. Simple houses – some have always stood on this site, others were brought in from elsewhere – contain personal possessions, illustrating both how much the migrants brought with them, and how much the different groups

▼ CENTRAL OAHU PLANTATION-ERA HOUSE

PLACES Central Oahu

▲ DOLE PLANTATION

shared with each other in creating a common Hawaiian identity. Cumulatively, the minor domestic details – pots, pans, buckets, family photographs, even the tiny boxing gloves used to train Filipino fighting cocks – make you feel the occupants have merely stepped out for a minute. The most moving artifacts in the museum are the *bangos*, the numbered metal badges that helped the *lunas* (whip-cracking Caucasian plantation supervisors) to distinguish each worker from the next. Goods could be obtained in the company store by showing your *bango*, the cost of which was deducted from your next pay packet.

Wahiawā

All routes across central Oahu – whether you take H-2 or Kamehameha Highway from Pearl City, or the more scenic Kunia Road that leads up through the fields from Waipahu – have to pass through the large town of Wahiawā in the heart of the island. The main drag holds the dismal array of bars, fast-food outlets, and gun stores that you'd expect to find this close to the Schofield Barracks, Oahu's largest military base (which by all accounts is actually very pretty, if you can get through the gates).

A couple of mildly diverting sites lie just outside the town.

The Wahiawā Botanical Gardens (daily 9am–4pm; free), a mile east, is a reasonably attractive enclave of tropical trees and flowers that's welcome if you live here but nothing special by Hawaiian standards. To the north, on Whitmore Avenue off Kamehameha Highway, faintly marked reddish-brown lava boulders beneath a cluster of palm trees in a pineapple field constitute an archeological site known as Kukaniloko, or more colloquially as the Birthing Stones. Tradition had it that any chief hoping to rule Oahu had to be born here.

Dole Plantation

Kamehameha Hwy, Wahiawā. Daily 9am–5.30pm; admission free. Gardens adults $3.75, under-13s $3, on foot, or adults $7.50, under-13s $5.50, by train. Maze adults $5.50, under-13s $3; Ⓦ www.dole-plantation .com. The single-story modern building of the Dole Plantation stands to the east of Kamehameha Highway roughly a mile north of Wahiawā. Though the large number of cars and tour buses parked outside might lead you to expect something more interesting, the plantation is basically a large covered mall-cum-marketplace, as described below. At least, should you so wish, you can take uproarious photographs of yourself with your head poking through a cardboard cutout of a pineapple playing a ukulele.

Behind the mall, extensive gardens of pineapples and more authentic Hawaiian plants can be explored either on foot or on half-hourly excursions on the Pineapple Express motorized "train." A separate section holds what the *Guinness Book of Records* considers to be the world's largest maze, again composed of Hawaiian plants. The aim here is not to reach the center, let alone escape; instead you're expected to traipse around in the hot sun to find six separate color-coded "stations."

Shops

Dole Plantation Store

Dole Plantation, Kamehameha Hwy, Wahiawā ⓦ www.dole-plantation.com. Daily 9am–5.30pm. As you might expect, almost all the stock in this large roadside store is in some way pineapple-related. If you can handle that, it's not that bad, though a taste for kitsch clearly helps. Besides souvenirs and craft items, *aloha* shirts with pineapple motifs and soft-toy pineapples with arms, legs and cheeky grins, they also sell fresh pineapples and pineapple products such as juices and frozen "whips."

Leeward Oahu

The west or leeward coast of Oahu, cut off from the rest of the island behind the Wai'anae mountains, is only accessible via Farrington Highway (H-93), which skirts the southern end of the ridge. Customarily dismissed as arid, the region may not be covered by tropical vegetation, but the scenery is still spectacular. As elsewhere on Oahu, the mountains are pierced by high green valleys – almost all of them inaccessible to casual visitors – while fine beaches such as Mākaha Beach Park line the shore.

The strip development that characterizes both sides of H-1 from Honolulu to Waipahu finally comes to an end as you enter the southwest corner of Oahu. Long-cherished plans by the state authorities to turn this region into a major tourism and residential center seem finally to be approaching fruition, however, as the former plantation settlement of 'Ewa becomes ever more overshadowed by the burgeoning modern community of Kapolei.

Further on, on the leeward coast proper, the traditionally minded inhabitants of towns such as *Nānākuli* are not disposed to welcome the encroachment of hotels and golf courses, and visitors tend to be treated with a degree of suspicion. The further north you go, the stronger the military presence becomes, with soldiers in camouflage lurking in the hillsides, and helicopters flying overhead.

'Ewa

A couple of miles south of Farrington Highway along Fort Weaver Road, 'Ewa is a picturesque little hamlet of wooden sugar-plantation homes arranged around a well-kept village green. Other than snapping a few photos along the back lanes, the only reason to come here is to take a train excursion with the Hawaii Railway Society, based just west of town along Renton Road. Their souvenir store and museum is open all week (Mon–Sat 9am–3pm, Sun 10am–3pm; free), but only on Sunday afternoons does the restored *Waialua #6* locomotive set out on its ninety-minute round-trip journey westwards to Kahe Point (1pm & 3pm; adults $10, seniors & under-13s $7; ☎808/681-5461, ⓦ www.hawaiianrailway.com). On the second Sunday of each month, at the same times but by reservation only, you can have a private narrated tour in the comfort of a restored luxury parlor car ($15).

'Ewa Beach Park

'Ewa Beach Park, three miles south of the village, is an

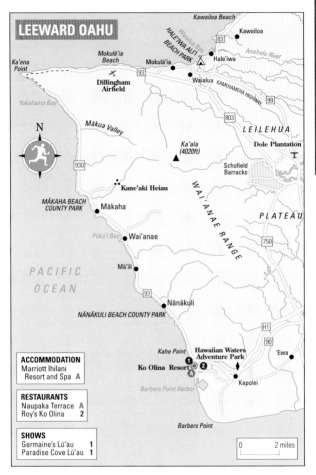

LEEWARD OAHU

ACCOMMODATION
Marriott Ihilani
Resort and Spa **A**

RESTAURANTS
Naupaka Terrace **A**
Roy's Ko Olina **2**

SHOWS
Germaine's Lū'au **1**
Paradise Cove Lū'au **1**

attractive oceanfront park popular with sailors from the nearby base. It has plenty of sand, and views across to Diamond Head, but the water tends to be too murky for swimming, and there's an awful lot of seaweed around.

Hawaiian Waters Adventure Park

400 Farrington Hwy, Kapolei. Hours vary; adults $35, ages 4–11 $25; ☎808/674-9283, ⒲www .hawaiianwaters.com. Until

recently, the name Kapolei did not appear on even the most detailed maps of Oahu. Now, however, it's the island's fastest-growing town, stretching alongside H-1 as the road approaches its end in the southwest corner of the island. Homes, movie theatres, and shopping malls have sprung up at an astonishing rate, but the new town has so far made only one bid to attract tourists, in the shape of the Hawaiian Waters

▲ HAWAIIAN WATERS ADVENTURE PARK

Adventure Park, just off exit 1 from H-1.

Hawaii's first water park follows the model of its predecessors in California, Florida, and elsewhere, with lots of swirling plastic tubes for visitors to raft or simply slide down, children's play areas, and an exhilarating wave pool. It's all great fun, though with so many wonderful beaches on the island to compete with, it hasn't yet succeeded in attracting great numbers of visitors. In principle, it's open daily from 10.30am until dusk, but it often seems to shut its gates as early as 4pm, and it's closed altogether some days in winter; call ahead before you make the drive.

Ko Olina Resort

A great deal of money was poured during the 1980s into landscaping the Ko Olina Resort, just north of Barbers Point at the southwest tip of the island. Four successive artificial lagoons were blasted into the coastline, each a perfect semicircle and equipped with its own crescent of white sand. Work also began on creating a marina

for luxury yachts at the Barbers Point Harbor. However, apart from the *Marriott Ihilani Resort*, reviewed on p.175, very few of the other projected developments, which were supposed to include residential estates, condo buildings, shopping centers, and more hotels, have so far materialized. Its chief neighbors, the relentlessly tacky *lū'au* sites belonging to *Paradise Cove* and *Germaine's* (see p.161), are something of a poor relation.

▼ KO OLINA RESORT

Nānākuli

Farrington Highway reaches the Wai'anae coast at Kahe Point Beach Park, near the section known as "Tracks" because of the adjacent railroad tracks. As well as being a small but pretty strip of sand, this is Oahu's most popular year-round surfing site. The waves offshore remain high (but not overpoweringly so) even in summer, and break much closer to the shore than usual. Since the bay itself is relatively sheltered, swimming usually only becomes dangerous in the depths of winter.

A couple of miles further on, Nānākuli is the southernmost of a string of small coastal towns. According to local legends, its name means either "look at knee" or "pretend to be deaf" – neither of which seems to make much sense. The population is largely Hawaiian, and there's little attempt to cater to outsiders. Nānākuli Beach Park, which runs alongside the highway all through town, is another good summer swimming beach, while Zablan Beach at its southern end is much used by scuba divers. The beach immediately north of *Nānākuli* is called Ulehawa or "filthy penis," after a particularly unsavory ancient chief.

Wai'anae

Wai'anae, five miles up the coast from Nānākuli, centers on curving Poka'i Bay. Thanks to the breakwaters constructed to protect the boat harbor at its northern end, the main sandy beach here is the only one on the leeward coast where swimming can be guaranteed safe all year round. An irresistible backdrop is provided by the high-walled valley behind.

Beyond a flourishing coconut grove at the tip of the flat spit of land that marks the southern end of Poka'i Bay stand the ruined walls of Kū'ilioloa Heiau. Unusual in being virtually surrounded by water, this three-tiered structure is said to mark the place where the first coconut tree to be brought from Tahiti was planted in Hawaiian soil. Kamehameha offered sacrifices here before launching his first invasion attempt against Kauai.

Mākaha

Mākaha, or "savage," the last of the leeward towns, was once the hideout of a dreaded band of outlaws. Now famous for the savagery of its waves, it began to attract surfers in the early 1950s. Before World War II, virtually all Oahu surfing was concentrated in Waikīkī. When changes in the ocean conditions there, and the development of new techniques and equipment led surfers to start looking elsewhere, Mākaha was the first place they hit on. The waves at its northern end are said to be the largest consistently reliable surf in Hawaii, and several major surfing contests are still held at Mākaha Beach Park each year. In summer, when sand piles up in mighty drifts, it's often possible to swim here in safety, and Mākaha retains enough sand to remain a beautiful crescent beach even in winter.

You'll probably notice what look like hotels along the oceanfront near Mākaha Beach, but they're all long-term rental condos intended for local families. With a county permit, however (see p.174), it's possible to camp at Kea'au Beach Park, in an attractive but somewhat exposed location another couple of miles up the coast, in view of Ka'ena Point. Swimming in the rocky sea here, with its pounding surf, is not recommended, but

▲ MĀKAHA BEACH

the numbered campsites are pleasant enough.

Kāne'āki Heiau

Mauna Olu Estates, Mākaha. Tues–Sun 10am–2pm; free. A couple of miles back from the ocean in Mākaha Valley – follow Mākaha Valley Road inland beyond the defunct *Sheraton Mākaha Resort*, and the astonishingly ugly Mākaha Towers apartment blocks that disfigure the northern side of the valley – the private driveway of the Mauna Olu Estates leads to Kāne'āki Heiau. The most thoroughly restored ancient temple in Hawaii, it was excavated by Bishop Museum archeologists in 1970 and can now be visited with permission from the security guards at the gate; you'll have to leave a drivers' license or passport as surety. Its principal platform of weathered, lichen-covered stones is topped once more by authentic thatched structures such as the *anu'u* ("oracle tower"), as well as carved images of the gods. The *heiau* originated as an agricultural temple to the god Lono in the fifteenth century. Two hundred years later, around the time of Kamehameha the Great, it was

converted into a *luakini*, where human sacrifices were dedicated to the god Ku – a typical progression indicating that the valley had come to support a large enough population to have its own paramount chief.

The road to Ka'ena Point

Beyond Mākaha, the highway traces a long, slow curve up the coast to Yokohama Bay. Barely populated, and splendidly bleak, this region attracts very few visitors other than a handful of daredevil surfers prepared to risk its sharks, currents, and mighty waves.

Inland, the rolling green slopes of Mākua Valley also conceal dangerous secrets. Used by the Air Force for bombing practice during and after World War II, the valley is still barred to the public owing to unexploded ordnance. Gaping Kāneana Cave to the south is too vandalized to be worth investigating.

Not even the sturdiest 4WD vehicle could negotiate the dirt road that continues from the end of the highway. In any case, the dunes beyond were designated as the Ka'ena Point Natural Area Reserve to help repair damage done by military jeeps and motorbikes. However, an

▲ ALBATROSS NESTING AT KA'ENA POINT

exposed one-hour hike along the route of the old railroad tracks will bring you to the very tip of the island. The walk is substantially similar to the corresponding trail along the North Shore, described on p.148.

Restaurants

Naupaka Terrace

Marriott Ihilani Resort and Spa, 92-1001 Olani St, Ko Olina Resort, Kapolei ☎ 808/679-0079. Daily 6.30am–10pm. Though the *Naupaka Terrace* is the least formal, and least expensive, of the *Ihilani Resort*'s in-house restaurants, its poolside setting is still spectacular, as indeed are the prices, from the $27 breakfast buffet onwards (a "Healthy Start" costs $19). Dinner will set you back at least $50, though the delicate Pacific Rim fish dishes are well worth trying.

Roy's Ko Olina

92-1220 Aliinui Drive, Ko Olina Resort, Kapolei ☎ 808/676-7697. Mon–Thurs & Sun 11am–9.30pm,

Fri & Sat 11am–10pm. Beautifully located outlet of the upscale Pacific Rim chain, overlooking the Ko Olina Golf Club, and serving the same range of exquisite Asian-influenced dishes as the Hawaii Kai branch, described on p.127.

Shows

Germaine's

Ko Olina Resort, Kapolei ☎ 808/949-6626 or 1-800/367-5655, ⓦ www .germainesluau.com. Adults $65, ages 14–20 $55, ages 6–13 $45. Nightly, 6pm. *Germaine's* and its neighbor and rival *Paradise Cove* are the two biggest *lū'aus* on Oahu. You'll see them advertised everywhere, and should be able to find discount tickets through "activity centers" in Waikīkī. What their ads don't make clear, however, is that both take place in the Ko Olina Resort, thirty miles from Waikīkī in the far southwestern corner of the island. The price includes an hour-long bus trip each way; be prepared for an interminable wait at either end of your trip for pick-ups and drop-offs from what feels like every hotel in Waikīkī, and for communal singalongs en route. Your reward at the end is the chance to spend hours looking at tacky, overpriced souvenirs, eating bland food, drinking weak cocktails, and watching third-rate entertainment.

Paradise Cove

Ko Olina Resort, Kapolei ☎ 808/842-5911 or 1-800/775-2683, ⓦ www .paradisecove.com. Adults $73, ages 13–18 $63, ages 4–12 $53. Nightly 6pm. Very much the same experience as described above for *Germaine's*, but a bit worse. Pretty enticing, eh?

Accommodation

Accommodation

The overwhelming majority of visitors to Oahu stay in the resort enclave of Waikīkī, a couple of miles east of central Honolulu. According to official statistics, the average room in Waikīkī costs $155 per night. There's a heavy premium for oceanfront accommodation, however, and away from the beach – bearing in mind that nowhere in Waikīkī is more than a few minutes' walk from the sea – it's easy enough to find something for around half that. Except for the very top-of-the-line properties, there's little point choosing a hotel with a swimming pool – most are squeezed onto rooftop terraces, overlooked by thousands of rooms in the surrounding high-rises and attracting all the dirt and fumes of the city. The sheer quantity of rooms ensures that you're unlikely to find yourself stranded if you arrive without a reservation, and several hostels cater to budget travelers.

Honolulu itself holds a handful of hotels, but there are very few alternatives in the rest of the island; the only hotels are the *Turtle Bay Resort* and Ihilani resorts, at the far northeast and southwest corners respectively, while the bargain *Backpackers Vacation Inn*, on the North Shore, caters to the surf crowd. Other than a few tiny B&Bs at Kailua and Kāneʻohe on the windward coast, that's about it.

Waikīkī

Budget hotels

Aloha Punawai 305 Saratoga Rd ☏808/923-5211 or 1-866/713-9694, ⓦ www.alternative-hawaii.com/alohapunawai/. Miniature hotel, opposite the post office, whose 19 studios and apartments are furnished in a crisp Japanese style and start at $110 per night. All units are air-conditioned, with kitchens, bathrooms, balconies, and TV, but no phones; only the slightly pricier "deluxe" options will sleep three guests. Small discounts for weekly stays.

Aqua Continental 2426 Kūhiō Ave ☏808/922-2232 or 1-866/406-2782, ⓦ www.aquaresorts.com. Plain but very presentable refurbished rooms from $92 per night, in a 27-story high-rise in the heart of Waikīkī, two blocks back from the beach; no balconies, and very few ocean views.

The Breakers 250 Beach Walk ☏808/923-3181 or 1-800/426-0494, ⓦ www.breakers-hawaii.com. Small, intimate, air-conditioned hotel on the western edge of central Waikīkī, close to the beach. All its two-person studio apartments (from $125) and four-person garden suites (from $185) have kitchenettes, phones, and TV, there's a bar and grill beside the flower-surrounded pool, and there's even a Japanese teahouse. Limited free parking.

Hawaiian King 417 Nohonani St ☏808/922-3894 or 1-800/247-1903, ⓦ www.hawaiianking-hotel.com. Each room in this venerable low-rise condo hotel, three blocks back from the beach in central Waikīkī, is privately owned, so they differ considerably, and they're not especially fancy, but all have kitchen, a/c and balcony. $139 per night, with discounted weekly and monthly rates.

Hawaiiana Hotel 260 Beach Walk ☏808/923-3811 or 1-800/367-5122, ⓦ www.hawaiianahotelatwaikiki.com. Abounding with *tiki* statues and the like, this pleasant low-rise family hotel, close to the beach and central Waikīkī, is the most appealing of the budget options in the area, with rates from $125. All the rooms, arranged around two pools, have

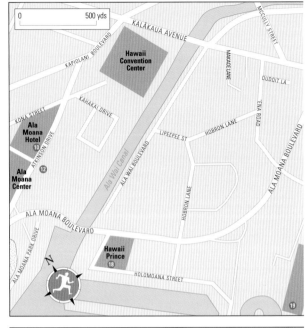

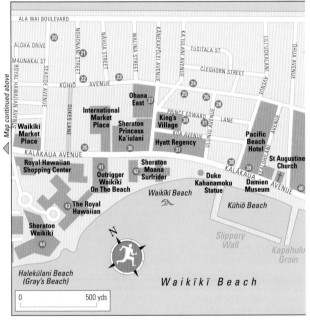

167

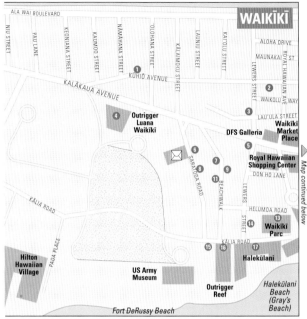

Map continued below

ACCOMMODATION

Ala Moana Hotel	10	Ohana Waikīkī West	23
Aloha Punawai	6	Outrigger Luana Waikīkī	4
Aqua Bamboo & Spa	24	Outrigger Reef	16
Aqua Continental	25	Outrigger Regency on Beachwalk	9
Aqua Island Colony	20	Outrigger Waikīkī on the Beach	41
Cabana at Waikīkī	29	Outrigger Waikīkī Shore	15
Central Branch YMCA	12	Pacific Beach Hotel	39
Halekūlani	17	Pacific Ohana	32
Hale Aloha Hostel		Polynesian Hostel Beach Club	34
(Hostelling International		ResortQuest Pacific Monarch	26
Waikīkī)	30	ResortQuest Waikīkī Circle Hotel	38
Hawaiian King	21	ResortQuest Waikīkī Joy	3
Hawaiiana Hotel	7	Royal Grove	28
Hawaii Prince	18	Sheraton Moana Surfrider	42
Hilton Hawaiian Village	19	Sheraton Princess Ka'iulani	36
Hyatt Regency	37	Sheraton Waikīkī	44
Ilima Hotel	22	The Breakers	11
Imperial of Waikīkī	14	The Royal Hawaiian	43
Kai Aloha	8	Waikīkī Beach Marriott	40
Ohana East	27	Waikīkī Beachside	
Ohana Islander Waikīkī	5	Hotel & Hostel	33
Ohana Maile Sky Court	1	Waikīkī Parc	13
Ohana Waikīkī Beachcomber	35	Waikīkī Prince	31
Ohana Waikīkī Malia	2		

kitchenettes, some have *lānais*, and they're equipped to varying degrees of luxury.

Kai Aloha 235 Saratoga Rd ☏808/923-6723, ⊛http://kaialoha.magicktravel .com/. Tiny, very central hotel, with *lānai* studios from $76 and apartments from $85 that sleep up to four, all with kitchenettes, bathrooms, TV, and air-conditioning.

Ohana East, 150 Kaʻiulani Ave ☏808/922-5353 or 1-800/462-6262, ⊛www.ohanahotels.com. While the rooms – and the bathrooms – here are on the small side, the staff and services are as good as you'd expect of the Ohana chain, and the convenient location, a block back from the beach and very close to several good restaurants, makes it a very dependable option, especially for budget-conscious families. Typical rates start at $149.

Royal Grove 151 Uluniu Ave ☏808/923-7691, ⊛www.royalgrovehotel.com. Small-scale, family-run hotel with a homey feel in central Waikīkī. The facilities improve the more you're prepared to pay, but even the most basic rooms, which lack air-conditioning and cost from $64 per night, are of a reliable standard, albeit undeniably faded, and hold two beds. There's also a courtyard pool – making the *Royal Grove* one of Waikīkī's best bets for budget travelers – a piano for guest use, and all sorts of retro bric-a-brac scattered around the shared spaces. Special weekly rates apply April–Nov only.

Waikīkī Prince 2431 Prince Edward St ☏808/922-1544, ⊛www.waikikiprince .com. Slightly drab but perfectly adequate and very central budget hotel (not to be confused with the upscale *Hawaii Prince Hotel Waikīkī*; see p.170). All rooms have air-conditioning, en-suite baths, and basic cooking facilities, but no phones; the "very small" and "small" categories, which start at under $70, are cheaper than "economy" units, while "standard" is top of the range. Office open 9am–6pm only; seventh night free April–Nov.

Mid-range hotels

Aqua Bamboo & Spa 2425 Kūhiō Ave ☏808/922-7777 or 1-866/406-2782, ⊛http://aquaresorts.com/. Very central, very stylish "boutique hotel," two blocks back from the beach, and holding twelve stories but less than a hundred rooms, all of which have appealing furnishings and live plants, with at least one *lānai*, plus free high-speed Internet and a large-screen LCD TV. Rates start at $118.

Aqua Island Colony 445 Seaside Ave ☏808/923-2345 or 1-866/406-2782, ⊛http://aquaresorts.com/. Anonymous-looking 44-story high-rise at the quieter inland side of Waikīkī, still around five minutes' walk from the beach. Despite the name, it holds conventional hotel rooms, from $102, as well as more luxurious suites from $133; all are furnished to a high standard and have their own balconies, though many of the bathrooms are small.

Cabana at Waikīkī 2551 Cartwright Rd ☏808/926-5555 or 1-877/902-2121, ⊛www.cabana-waikiki.com. Boutique hotel, charging over the odds because it's heavily geared towards gay men. All its 19 nice but not exquisite mini-suites, priced from $149, hold kitchenettes and extra daybeds, and guests get free breakfasts, plus free cocktails some nights. There's a small, clothes-optional outdoor hot tub.

Ilima Hotel 445 Nohonani St ☏808/923-1877, 1-800/801-9366 (HI) or 1-800/367-5172 (US & Canada), ⊛www.ilima.com. Good-value small hotel, near the canal on the *mauka* side of central Waikīkī and catering to a mainly local clientele. The spacious condo units each offer two double beds, a kitchen, additional sofabeds, and free local calls, and there's limited free parking. Prices start at $177, but there are good discounts for seniors and AAA members.

Imperial of Waikīkī 205 Lewers St ☏808/923-1827 or 1-800/347-2582 (US & Canada), ⊛www .imperialofwaikiki.com. Studio rooms and one- or two-bedroom balcony suites in a tower block set slightly back from the beach, just south of Kalākaua Avenue; online rates start at $138. A bit hemmed in by the oceanfront giants, but not bad for groups traveling together. The best views are from the terrace around the 27th floor pool.

Outrigger Luana Waikīkī 2045 Kalākaua Ave ☏808/955-6000 or 1-800/445-8811,

Outrigger and Ohana hotels

The family-oriented **Outrigger** chain currently runs eleven hotels in Waikīkī, divided into two separate categories to convey their differences. Five of the most luxurious carry the Outrigger brand name, while the rest are **Ohana** (which means "family" in Hawaiian) hotels.

Outrigger has been moving consistently upmarket in recent years, most obviously by spearheading the redevelopment of the Beachwalk area. Several of its older properties have closed, while new additions include the *Regency on Beachwalk* and the *Luana Waikīkī*. Nonetheless, by Waikīkī standards, all the Outrigger and Ohana properties remain competitively priced. Even the oceanfront *Outrigger Waikīkī On The Beach* is less opulent than places like the *Royal Hawaiian* or the *Hilton Hawaiian Village*, and costs significantly less per night. You can expect to find Internet rates for all the Ohana properties of under $150 per night, and for that you'll get a clean, well-maintained room with standard but smart hotel furnishings.

A high proportion of Outrigger and Ohana guests are on all-inclusive vacation packages. If you contact either chain directly, or access their websites, look for special offers, and especially their plethora of room-and-car deals. Standard room rates, however, remain constant year-round; where the price codes below indicate ranges, these refer to the best available online rates for a standard double room with and without ocean views. Most properties hold more expensive suites.

Outrigger hotels

* *Luana Waikīkī*, 2045 Kalākaua Ave
Reef, 2169 Kālia Rd
Regency on Beachwalk,
  255 Beachwalk
**Waikīkī On The Beach*,
  2335 Kalākaua Ave
Waikīkī Shore, 2161 Kālia Rd

Outrigger reservations

ⓦ www.outrigger.com
US & Canada ☎ 1-800/688-7444
Worldwide ☎ 303/369-7777

* see detailed review in main listings

Ohana hotels

* *East*, 150 Ka'iulani Ave
Islander Waikīkī, 270 Lewers St
Maile Sky Court, 2058 Kūhiō Ave
Waikīkī Beachcomber,
  2300 Kalākaua Ave
Waikīkī Malia, 2211 Kūhiō Ave
Waikīkī West, 2330 Kūhiō Ave

Ohana reservations

ⓦ www.ohanahotels.com
US & Canada ☎ 1-800/462-6262
Worldwide ☎ 303/369-7777

ⓦ www.outrigger.com. Smart, totally remodeled condo block, back from the beach at the western end of Waikīkī, that's become one of the jewels in the Outrigger chain. Characterful, individually styled kitchenette studios and hotel rooms, with an upscale Hawaiian flavor, from $195 to $325 per night.

Pacific Beach Hotel 2490 Kalākaua Ave ☎ 808/922-1233, 923-4511 or 1-800/367-6060, ⓦ www.pacificbeachhotel .com. The *Pacific Beach* has 830 rooms in two separate towers, at the Diamond Head end of Kalākaua Avenue, and also offers a pool, ocean-view spa, and tennis facilities. The high central tower contains the Oceanarium – a three-story fish tank that's the focus for diners in the *Oceanarium* restaurant (see p.57). Best rates online, from $185.

ResortQuest Pacific Monarch 2427 Kūhiō Ave ☎ 808/923-9805 or 1-866/774-2924, ⓦ www.pacific-monarch .com. Tall condo building in the heart of Waikīkī holding small studios with kitchenettes, plus larger four-person suites with full kitchens and *lānais*, and a rooftop swimming pool. Online rates start as low as $148.

ResortQuest Waikīkī Circle Hotel 2464 Kalākaua Ave ☎808/923-1571 or 1-877/997-6667, ⊛www .resortquesthawaii.com. Bright and cheery turquoise-and-white octagonal tower, dwarfed by its surroundings but one of the cheapest options along the oceanfront. Each of its thirteen circular floors is divided into eight identical rooms with two double beds and a *lānai*; prices vary according to how much sea you can see. The hotel is the base for Aloha Express Tours; see p.184. Look for rates from $129 online.

ResortQuest Waikīkī Joy 320 Lewers St ☎808/923-2300 or 1-877/997-6667, ⊛www.resortquesthawaii.com. Friendly, good-value little hotel, with quirky though dated pastel-trimmed decor, from the airy garden lobby through to the faded but perfectly adequate rooms, which cost from $125 and feature whirlpool baths and incongruous retro hi-fi systems. Free continental breakfast, plus a café and even a karaoke bar. $100–150.

Sheraton Princess Ka'iulani 120 Ka'iulani Ave ☎808/922-5811 or 1-866/500-8313, ⊛www.princess -kaiulani.com. Ugly tower-block hotel, with drab, old-fashioned public spaces and well over a thousand rooms, usually packed with vacationing families. Not quite on the seafront but big enough to command wide views of the ocean (rooms from $175) and mountains (from $140). The tiny street-level pool is somewhat marred by traffic noise.

Waikīkī Parc 2233 Helumoa Rd ☎808/921-7272 or 1-800/422-0450, ⊛www.waikikiparc.com. Modern high-rise set slightly back from the beach, operated by the same management as the *Halekūlani* opposite, and offering a taste of the same luxury at significantly more affordable prices, though recent renovations have increased rates significantly. Very tastefully decorated top-of-the-line rooms, plus the superb *Nobu* restaurant (see p.57). City views from $164, ocean views from $220.

Expensive hotels

Halekūlani 2199 Kālia Rd ☎808/923-2311 or 1-800/367-2343, ⊛www .halekulani.com. Stunning oceanfront hotel, arranged around an exquisite courtyard and pool, in a prime location for views along the beach to Diamond Head, but aloof from the resort bustle. Probably the most luxurious option in Waikīkī – even if you opt for the cheapest, $405 room, rather than the $5000-per-night Vera Wang honeymoon suite, you'll have a huge room with *lānai*, a deep bath and walk-in shower, and DVD player. It's also home to the highly rated *Orchids* (see p.58) and *La Mer* restaurants, while the open-air *House Without a Key* bar (see p.60) is perfect for sunset cocktails.

Hawaii Prince Hotel Waikīkī 100 Holomoana St ☎808/956-1111 or 1-888/977-4623, ⊛www .princeresortshawaii.com. Extremely classy Japanese-styled hotel, overlooking the yacht harbor and just a short walk from the Ala Moana shopping mall (which makes it a long walk from Waikīkī proper). Its twin towers have spacious and very comfortable rooms with floor-to-ceiling ocean views (though not *lānais*), plus two good restaurants, and it even has its own golf course, albeit half an hour's drive away. Look for good deals online, from $219 per night.

Hilton Hawaiian Village 2005 Kālia Rd ☎808/949-4321 or 1-800/445-8667, ⊛www.hawaiianvillage.hilton.com. With 3400 rooms and counting, the *Hilton* is the largest hotel in Hawaii and the largest non-casino hotel in the US (the second largest in the world). It's a scaled-down version of all Waikīkī, holding a hundred of the exact same stores and restaurants you'd find out on the streets. The center of Waikīkī is a 15min walk away, and since there's a good pool, a great stretch of beach (see p.49), and even a lagoon populated by penguins and flamingos, there's little incentive to leave the hotel precincts – which is, of course, the point. Expect to pay from $249 for a garden view, and $299 for an ocean view, while even self-parking costs $20 per night.

Hyatt Regency Waikīkī Resort And Spa
2424 Kalākaua Ave ☎808/923-1234 or
1-866/333-8881, ⊛http://waikiki.hyatt
.com. Very lavish, very central property,
across the road from the heart of Waikīkī
Beach, and consisting of two enormous
towers engulfing a central atrium equipped
with cascading waterfalls and tropical
vegetation. Also holds an upmarket
shopping mall, an open-air pool, 1230
"oversized" rooms, a spa, and nine
restaurants, of which two, *Ciao Mein* and
The Colony, are reviewed on pp.55–56.
Online rates start at $233 for a "city view,"
$308 for an ocean view.

Outrigger Waikīkī On The Beach 2335
Kalākaua Ave ☎808/923-0711 or
1-800/688-7444, ⊛www.outrigger.com.
Flagship Outrigger hotel, in prime position
close to the center of Waikīkī Beach, with
good restaurants and entertainment. The
rooms closest to the ocean offer great
views and facilities, including huge whirlpool
baths; those further back are less special,
but the rates are very reasonable for such a
choice location. You can hope to find online
rates of $239 for a city view, $299 for an
ocean view.

The Royal Hawaiian 2259 Kalākaua Ave
☎808/923-7311 or 1-866/716-8109,
⊛www.royal-hawaiian.com. The 1920s
"Pink Palace" (see p.51), now owned by
Sheraton, remains one of Waikīkī's best-
loved landmarks. The atmospheric original
building, which seeps vintage glamor, still
commands a great expanse of beach and
looks over a lawn to the sea; pink through
and through, it remains a lovely place to
hang out, with elegant rooms and peaceful
gardens at the back. Sadly, though, it's now
flanked by a less atmospheric tower block
holding additional suites. Includes a full-
service spa. On Monday, a *lū'au* is held on
the ocean-facing lawn (see p.61). Expect to
pay just under $300 for a garden view, from
$379 for an oceanfront room.

Sheraton Moana Surfrider 2365
Kalākaua Ave ☎808/922-3111 or
1-866/716-8109, ⊛www.moana
-surfrider.com. Waikīkī's oldest hotel, built
at the end of the nineteenth century (see
p.50). Despite extensive restoration, the
"Colonial" architectural style of the original

building – now the focus of the Banyan
wing – remains intact, though these days
it's flanked by two huge towers. The main
lobby, with its tongue-and-groove walls,
memorabilia cabinets, soothing sea breezes
and old-time atmosphere, is a delight
– prepare yourself to pick through countless Japanese wedding parties – and the
beachfront setting, with its broad verandah
and colossal banyan tree, is unsurpassed.
Many of the actual rooms, however, are
surprisingly faded and worn. The cheapest
city-view rooms start at $250, ocean views
from $330.

Waikīkī Beach Marriott Resort & Spa
2552 Kalākaua Ave ☎808/922-6611
or 1-800/367-5370, ⊛www
.marriottwaikiki.com. This huge, totally
renovated property consists of two giant
towers facing the eastern end of Waikīkī
Beach; while not historic, it has a stylish,
contemporary Hawaiian feel, and offers
Waikīkī's best value at the top end of the
spectrum. As well as a state-of-the-art
spa, it holds several excellent restaurants,
including the wonderful *Sansei* (see p.58),
while the *Moana Terrace* hosts superb
Hawaiian musicians (see p.61). City views
from $239, oceanviews from $299.

Hostels

**Hale Aloha Hostel (Hostelling
International Waikīkī)** 2417 Prince
Edward St ☎808/926-8313,
⊛www.hostelsaloha.com, ⓔayhaloha@
lava.net. Informal AYH-affiliated youth
hostel in the heart of Waikīkī, in a turquoise
four-story building a couple of minutes from
the beach. Dorm beds in four-person rooms
are $20 ($23 for non-members), while the
five double studio rooms cost $48 or $54;
guests share a kitchen and patio. Office
open 7am–3am; no curfew; seven-day max
stay. Reservations recommended, especially
for double rooms.

Pacific Ohana 2552 Lemon Rd
☎808/921-8111. The least appealing of
the Lemon Road hostels offers four-bed
dorms that share bathrooms for $20 per
person, and two-bed studios with bath and
kitchen for $75.

Polynesian Hostel Beach Club 2584
Lemon Rd ☎808/922-1340, ⊛www

.hawaiihostels.com. Former motel converted into a clean, safe, and efficient private hostel, a block from the sea at the Diamond Head end of Waikīkī. All the air-conditioned dorm rooms have en-suite bathrooms; some hold four bunk beds ($25 per person), some six ($23 per person), and some ten ($20). You can also get a "semi-private" room, sharing a bathroom, for $45 single, $54 double, or a studio for $67. Van tours of the island offered. Free use of snorkel gear and boogie boards, plus cheap bike and moped rental, and Internet access.

Waikīkī Beachside Hotel & Hostel 2556 Lemon Rd ☎808/923-9566, ⓦwww.waikikibeachsidehostel.com. By far the liveliest of the hostels along Lemon Road, near the park in eastern Waikīkī, and thus despite the name not actually "beachside." Beds in eight-person dorms cost $22.50, in four-person dorms $31.40; they also have "semi-private" double rooms, sharing bathroom and kitchen, for $67. It looks a smarter from the outside than it does once you go in, but it offers free continental breakfasts, a big-screen TV, Internet access, and snorkel and surf equipment rental.

Kapiʻolani Park and Diamond Head

New Otani Kaimana Beach Hotel 2863 Kalākaua Ave ☎808/923-1555 or 1-800/356-8264, ⓦwww.kaimana.com. Intimate Japanese-toned hotel, stylish and airy, on quiet and secluded Sans Souci Beach (see p.65). Half a mile east of the bustle of central Waikīkī, it boasts the lovely backdrop of Diamond Head. Its *Hau Tree Lanai* restaurant is reviewed on p.68. Valet parking only. Diamond Head views from $164, ocean views from $220.

W Honolulu 2885 Kalākaua Ave ☎808/922-1700 or 1-877/945-8357, ⓦwww.whotels.com. Very chic – some might say pretentious – hotel, part of an exclusive international chain, that's set a few yards back from the ocean just over half a mile east of Waikīkī (a condo tower blocks views from the lower stories). All

48 rooms have balconies (though some face Diamond Head rather than the ocean), CD players, and cordless phones, and the *Diamond Head Grill* restaurant (see p.68) is on the second floor. Rates start at $455.

Downtown Honolulu

ResortQuest at the Executive Center Hotel 1088 Bishop St ☎808/539-3000 or 1-877/997-6667, ⓦwww.resortquesthawaii.com. All-suite downtown hotel, enjoying great harbor views from the top of a forty-story skyscraper. Geared to business travelers, but the prices, from $230, compare well with similar standard Waikīkī hotels.

Waterfront Honolulu

Ala Moana Hotel 410 Atkinson Drive ☎808/955-4811, 1-800/446-8990 (HI) or 1-800/367-6025 (US & Canada), ⓦwww.alamoanahotel.com. Thousand-room tower block right alongside the Ala Moana Center, just down the road from the Convention Center, and five minutes' walk from Waikīkī. Managed by Outrigger, it consists of individually owned condo units, which vary but are generally of high standard. Though it's targeted primarily at business visitors and shopaholics, it offers the lively *Rumours* nightclub and some good restaurants, and there's an excellent beach close at hand (see p.91). Look for special rates online. Rooms from $119, suites from $279.

Best Western Plaza 3253 N Nimitz Highway ☎808/836-3636 or 1-800/800-4683, ⓦwww.bestwesternhonolulu.com. Large hotel fronting the highway, half a mile by free shuttle bus from the airport; like the nearby *Airport Hotel*, it's perfectly adequate for an exhausted layover between flights but convenient neither for the city nor the beach, and $145 for a room isn't particularly good value.

Central Branch YMCA 401 Atkinson Drive ☎808/941-3344, ⓦwww.ymcahonolulu.org. Set in attractive grounds opposite the Ala Moana shopping mall, just outside Waikīkī, with an on-site swimming pool and a beach nearby.

Accommodation includes plain rooms with shared bath for men only ($35 single/$46 double), plus some nicer en-suite doubles available to women too ($43 single/$59 double). All guests must reserve at least two weeks in advance, and have a definite check-out date; no walk-ins accepted.

Honolulu Airport Hotel 3401 N Nimitz Highway ☎808/836-0661 or 1-800/462-6262, ✆www.honoluluairporthotel.com. Three-hundred-room chain hotel, operated by Outrigger, close to the airport by a noisy freeway, and served by free 24-hour shuttles; the rooms are OK, but not cheap at $145, and it's not a place you'd spend more than one night.

Pagoda Hotel 1525 Rycroft St, Honolulu HI 96814 ☎808/941-6611 or 1-800/367-6060, ✆www.pagodahotel.com. This tower block, located within easy walking distance of Ala Moana mall, roughly halfway between downtown Honolulu and Waikīkī, is very much a budget rather than a fancy option. Conventional, if undeniably ageing, hotel rooms from just $90 per night, and one- and two-bedroom suites, plus two pools and a "floating restaurant."

Makiki and Mānoa

Fernhurst YWCA 1566 Wilder Ave ☎808/941-2231, ✆www.ywca.org. Women-only lodging, not far west of the University of Hawaii and quite a way from the ocean, that's intended primarily for locals in need. Double rooms share a bathroom with one other room, and cost $38 per person; some can be rented by single travelers for $48. Rates include simple buffet breakfasts and dinners; a $35 membership is compulsory.

Hosteling International Honolulu 2323-A Seaview Ave ☎808/946-0591, ✆http//hostelsaloha.com, ✉hihostel@lava.net. Youth hostel in a college residence in Mānoa, a couple of miles from Waikīkī. There's no direct bus from the airport: change at Ala Moana Center to TheBus #6 or #18; get off at Metcalfe Street/University Avenue, one block south of the hostel. Office hours 8am–noon and 4pm–midnight; no curfew. Beds

in the single-sex dorms (two are male, three female) cost $16 for AYH/IYHA members, $19 for nonmembers, while the private double room costs $42 and $48 respectively, with a three-night maximum stay for nonmembers.

Mānoa Valley Inn 2001 Vancouver Drive ☎808/947-6019, ✆www.manoavalleyinn.com. One of Honolulu's most relaxing options: a plush, antique-filled B&B inn, near the University of Hawaii in lush Mānoa Valley, with seven suites from $99 and one self-contained cottage for $175. Waikīkī feels a lot farther away than the mile it really is. Sit in one of the wicker chairs on the back porch and linger over breakfast.

Windward Oahu

Akamai B&B 172 Ku'umele Place, Kailua ☎808/261-2227 or 1-800/642-5366, ✉akamai@aloha.net. Homely little private B&B, in a quiet street very close to Kailua Beach, with two small, well-equipped en-suite units for under $100.

Ali'i Bluffs Windward B&B 46-125 Ikiiki St, Kāne'ohe ☎808/235-1124 or 1-800/235-1151, ✆www.hawaiiscene.com/aliibluffs. Small-scale B&B overlooking Kāne'ohe Bay, in a private antique-furnished home. There are two guest rooms, one with one double bed for $70, the other with two twin beds for $60. Each has a separate private bathroom, and there's a small swimming pool.

Kāne'ohe Bay B&B 45-302 Pu'uloko Place, Kāne'ohe ☎808/235-4214 or 1-800/262-9912, ✆www.bestbnb.com. Stylish, relaxing B&B in a magnificent setting beside Kāne'ohe Bay, available through the Hawaii's Best B&Bs. Guests enjoy use of a deck with good-sized swimming pool and Jacuzzi, and the hosts are absolute local experts. $150 per night.

Lā'ie Inn 55-109 Laniloa St, Lā'ie ☎808/293-9282 or 1-800/526-4562, ✆www.laieinn.com. Rather decrepid motel – anonymous and well away from the ocean, but reasonably inexpensive – less than a hundred yards north of the Polynesian Cultural Center. Rooms from

Camping on Oahu

You can **camp** in county parks on Oahu for free, and in state parks for $5 per night, with a permit from the relevant office. However, few sites are worth recommending, and none of those is especially convenient to Honolulu. Furthermore, all county and state campgrounds are closed on Wednesday and Thursday nights, and you can't stay at any one site for more than five days in one month. The best options among the **state parks** are those at Keaīwa Heiau (see p.151), Mālaekahana Bay (p.137), Waimānolo Bay (p.126), and Kahana Valley (p.134); appealing **county parks** include Bellows Field Beach (p.126), Kaiaka Bay Beach Park, a mile out of Hale'iwa near the mouth of Kaiaka Bay, and Kea'au Beach Park on the Leeward shore (p.159).

The **state parks office** accepts postal applications seven to thirty days in advance; it's located in Room 310, 1151 Punchbowl St, Honolulu HI 96813 (Mon–Fri 8.30am–3.30pm; ☎808/587-0300, ⊛www.hawaii.gov/dlnr/dsp). **County** permits can be obtained, in person only, from 650 S King St (Mon–Fri 7.45am–4pm; ☎808/523-4525, ⊛www.co.honolulu.hi.us/parks) or from the subsidiary "City Hall" in the Ala Moana Center (Mon–Fri 9am–4pm, Sat 8am–4pm; ☎808/973-2600).

$89; each has its own *lānai* overlooking the swimming pool.

Lanikai B&B 1277 Mokulua Drive, Kailua ☎808/261-1059 or 1-800/258-7895, ⊛www.lanikaibb.com. Spacious, old-fashioned home, across from Lanikai Beach, that offers a studio room facing the mountains for $145, a larger seaview apartment for $165, or a two-bedroom guest cottage for $200.

Sheffield House 131 Ku'ulei Rd, Kailua ☎808/262-0721, ⊛www .hawaiisheffieldhouse.com. Very hospitable B&B accommodation, in a private house just two minutes' walk from Kailua Beach. One guestroom, with a queen-size bed and private bath, costs $95 per night, or there's a two-room suite capable of sleeping four for $105.

The North Shore

Backpacker's Vacation Inn 59-788 Kamehameha Hwy, Pūpūkea ☎808/638-7838, ⊛www .backpackers-hawaii.com. The best budget option along the North Shore, *Backpacker's* was founded by Mark Foo, a daredevil Hawaiian surfer who died surfing in California in 1994. Its rambling main building, *mauka* of the highway, has dorm beds for $25 per night in high

season, and simple private double rooms sharing kitchen and bath for $65. Across the street, in low oceanfront buildings, good-value studio apartments with great views start at $125. The *Plantation Village*, a hundred yards down the road, across from the sea and run by the same management, consists of nine restored plantation cabins, with more dorm beds, plus private rooms and larger cabins at slightly higher rates. All rates are discounted for stays of a week or longer, and drop by ten percent between April and November. Communal buffet dinners on Tuesday, Wednesday, Friday, and Sunday cost $7, and there's a free daily bus to Honolulu Airport. They also provide free snorkeling equipment and boogie boards, rent out bicycles at $5 per day, offer Internet access at $8 per hour, and arrange island tours, plus whale watching in winter and scuba diving in summer.

Turtle Bay Resort 57-091 Kamehameha Hwy ☎808/293-6000 or 1-800/203-3650, ⊛www. turtlebayresort.com. This thousand-acre resort holds almost five hundred ocean-view rooms, as well as three swimming pools, a luxury spa, horse-riding facilities, two golf courses, ten tennis courts, a surf school, and three restaurants. Priced beyond the pockets of most of the surfing crowd, its presence is not very welcome with North Shore residents, who are forever campaigning to prevent its further expansion. If you're happy to pay rates that typically start at around $240 per night, though, it offers a truly fabulous resort experience, and makes a great escape from Waikiki.

Leeward Oahu

Marriott Ihilani Resort and Spa Ko Olina Resort 92-1001 Olani St, Kapolei

☏808/679-0079 or 1-800/626-4446, ⓦwww.ihilani.com. This largely successful attempt to mimic the resort hotels of the outer islands is an absolute idyll, if you can afford rates that usually start just under $300 online. The fifteen stories of state-of-the-art rooms are equipped with every high-tech device imaginable, from computerized lighting and air-conditioning systems to CD players and giant-screen TVs. The adjoining spa boasts thalassotherapy and sauna facilities, plus rooftop tennis courts and a top-quality golf course.

Essentials

Arrival

All **flights** to Oahu arrive at Honolulu's **International Airport**, five miles west of the downtown area, where the runways extend out to sea on a coral reef. The main **Overseas Terminal** is flanked by smaller **Inter-Island** and **Commuter** terminals, and connected to them by the free Wikiwiki shuttle service. All are located on a loop road, which is constantly circled by a wide array of hotel and rental-car pickup vans, taxis, and minibuses.

Virtually every arriving tourist heads straight to Waikīkī; if you don't have a **hotel or hostel reservation** use the courtesy phones in the baggage claim area, where you'll also find boards advertising room rates. Several competing **shuttle buses**, such as Airport Waikīkī Express (☎808/954-8652 or 1-866/898-2519, ⓦwww.robertshawaii .com; $9 one-way, $15 round-trip), Island Express (☎808/944-1879, ⓦhttp://islandexpresstransport.com;

$10 one-way, $19 round-trip), and Reliable Shuttle (☎808/924-9292, ⓦwww .reliableshuttle.com; $11 one-way, $19 round-trip), pick up regularly outside the terminals and will carry passengers to any Waikīkī hotel. A **taxi** from the airport to Waikīkī will cost $25–30, depending on traffic.

In addition, **TheBus** #19 and #20 run to Waikīkī from the airport, leaving from outside the Departures lounge of the Overseas Terminal. The ride costs $2 one-way, but you have to be traveling light: TheBus won't carry large bags, cases, or backpacks.

Car rental outlets abound; see below for advice on driving in Honolulu. The nine-mile – not at all scenic – **drive** from the airport to Waikīkī can take anything from 25 to 75 minutes. The quickest route is to follow H-1 as far as possible, running inland of downtown Honolulu, and then watch out for the Waikīkī exit.

Information

There are no visitor information centers worth visiting in Waikīkī or Honolulu. The best place to pick up brochures and printed material is the Arrivals hall at the airport, but almost every hotel runs its own information desk with further racks of brochures, and kiosks around Kalākaua Avenue offer greatly

discounted rates for island tours, helicopter rides, dinner cruises, surfing lessons, and so on. To get information in advance, access the websites of the **Hawaii Visitors Bureau (HVB)**; ☎808/923-1811 or 1-800/464-2924, ⓦwww.gohawaii.com) or the Island of Oahu (ⓦwww.visit-oahu.com).

Transportation

While renting a car enables you to explore Oahu in much greater depth, **driving** in Honolulu is not a pleasant

experience. The **traffic** on major roads, such as H-1 along the northern flanks of the city, and Likelike Highway and the

Pali Highway across the mountains, can be horrendous, and **parking** is always a problem. You may well find it easier to travel by **bus**, thanks to the exemplary TheBus network.

Buses

A network of over sixty **bus** routes, officially named TheBus and centered on downtown Honolulu and the Ala Moana shopping mall, covers the whole of Oahu (☎ 808/848-5555, ⊛ www .thebus.org). All journeys cost $2 (ages 6–17 $1), with free transfers to any connecting route if you ask as you board. The **4-Day Pass**, available from ABC stores in Waikīkī, offers four days' unlimited travel on TheBus for $20; monthly passes are also available, for $40. The most popular routes with Waikīkī-based tourists are **#2** to downtown, **#8** and **#58** to Ala Moana, **#19** and **#20** to the airport, **#20** and **#42** to Pearl Harbor, **#22** to Hanauma Bay, **#57** to Kailua and Kāne'ohe, and the bargain "**Circle Island**" buses that take four hours to tour Oahu, still for just $2: **#52** (clockwise) and **#55** (counterclockwise).

For tourists, the main alternative to TheBus is the ridiculously expensive **Waikīkī Trolley** (⊛ www.waikikitrolley .com; 1-day pass adults $25, ages 4–11 $12; 4-day pass adults $45, ages 4–11 $18), which runs open-sided trolleys on three separate lines. The **Red Line** tours from Waikīkī to Ala Moana, the waterfront, downtown Honolulu, Chinatown, and the Bishop Museum (every 45min; first departure *Hilton Hawaiian Village* 10am, terminates *Hawaii Prince* 6.26pm); the **Blue Line** connects Waikīkī with Sea Life Park by way of Diamond Head and Kahala Mall, but does not drop passengers at Hanauma Bay (hourly; first departure DFS Galleria 9am, terminates *Ohana Waikīkī West* 6.15pm); and the **Pink Line** simply shuttles between

Waikīkī and the Ala Moana Center (every 8min; first departure DFS Galleria 9.30am, terminates *Hilton Hawaiian Village* 8.04pm).

Car and bike rental

All the major **car rental** chains have outlets at the airport, and many have offices in Waikīkī as well. Reservations can be made using their national toll-free numbers and websites, but check first to see if you can get a better room-and-car deal through your hotel.

Bear in mind that Waikīkī hotels charge anything from $8 to $20 per night for **parking**, although there are meters on the back streets of Waikīkī, near the Ala Wai Canal. Downtown, the largest metered parking lot is on the edge of Chinatown at Smith and Beretania streets.

Lots of companies in and near Waikīkī rent out **bicycles**, **mopeds**, and **motorbikes**, including Adventure On Two Wheels, which adjoins the *Island Hostel* at 1946 Ala Moana Blvd (☎ 808/944-3131), and has another outlet at 2552 Lemon Rd (☎ 808/921-8111); Big Kahuna Rentals, 407 Seaside Ave (☎ 808/924-2736 or 1-888/451-5544, ⊛ www.bigkahunarentals.com); and the good-value Mopeds Direct, 750 Kapahulu Ave (☎ 808/732-3366). Typical rates for bikes are $15 per day (8am–6pm) or $20 for 24 hours; mopeds around $40 per day, or from $130 per week; and a Harley-Davidson motorbike will set you back perhaps $150 for a day, $750 for a week.

Taxis

Honolulu **taxi** firms include Charley's (☎ 808/531-1333, ⊛ www.charleystaxi .com), and TheCab (☎ 808/422-2222, ⊛ www.thecabhawaii.com). Handicabs of the Pacific (☎ 808/524-3866, ⊛ www .handicabs.com) provides transportation and tours for **disabled visitors**.

Money

Although it's possible to have an inexpensive vacation in Honolulu, prices in Hawaii are consistently higher than in the rest of the US. With 85 percent of the state's food and 92 percent of its fuel having to be shipped in, the cost of living is around forty percent above the US average.

How much you spend each day is, of course, up to you, but it's hard to get any sort of breakfast for under $8, a cheap lunch can easily come to $15, and an evening meal in a restaurant, with drinks, is likely to cost $30 or more per person, even if you're trying to economize. As outlined in the accommodation section, Waikīkī and Honolulu hold a number of hostels, which charge around $20 for a dorm bed, but otherwise even the cheapest hotels tend to charge over $80 a night for a double room, and a rental car with gas won't cost less than $30 a day. It's easy to spend $100 per person per day before you've done anything: pay for a snorkel cruise or a *lū'au*, and you've cleared $150.

The state **sales tax** of 4.17 percent on all transactions is almost never included in the prices displayed. Hotels impose an additional 7.25 percent tax, adding a total premium of more than eleven percent to accommodation bills.

Most visitors find that there's no reason to carry large amounts of cash or traveler's checks to Hawaii. Automatic teller machine (ATMs), which accept most cards issued by domestic and foreign banks, can be found almost everywhere; call your own bank if you're in any doubt. The two major banks are the Bank of Hawaii, which belongs to the Plus network of ATMs, and the First Hawaiian Bank, which belongs to the Plus and Cirrus networks. Even the smallest town tends to hold a branch of one or the other.

If you do want to take traveler's checks – which offer the great security of knowing that lost or stolen checks will be replaced – be sure to get them issued in US dollars. Foreign currency, whether cash or traveler's checks, can be hard to exchange, so foreign travelers should change some of their money into dollars at home.

For most services, it's taken for granted that you'll be paying with a credit card. Hotels and car rental companies routinely require an imprint of your card whether or not you intend to use it to pay.

Food and drink

Gone are the days when the Hawaiian Islands were self-sufficient Gardens of Eden; the state now produces less than twenty percent of the food it consumes, and in many ways eating in Oahu can be much like eating anywhere else in the US.

However, two important factors work in favor of visitors hoping for memorable culinary experiences. First of all, there's the island's ethnic diversity. Immigrants from all over the world have brought their own national dishes and recipes to Hawaii, and those separate traditions have repeatedly mingled to create intriguing new cuisines. Second, the presence of thousands of tourists, many prepared to pay top rates for good food, means that Honolulu in particular holds some truly superb fine dining restaurants, run by internationally renowned chefs.

Note that all restaurants are obliged by law to forbid smoking.

Local restaurants

Oahu has its fair share of outlets of the national fast-food chains, but locally owned budget restaurants, diners, and takeout stands serve a hybrid cuisine that draws on the traditions of Japan, China, Korea, and the Philippines as well as the US mainland. The resultant mixture has a slight but definite Hawaiian twist. In fact, the term "local" food has a distinct meaning in Hawaii, and specifically applies to this multicultural melange. The best place to find it in Honolulu is Chinatown, where the markets hold a fantastic array of options.

Breakfast tends to be the standard combination of eggs, meat, pancakes, muffins, or toast. At midday, the usual dish is the plate lunch, a molded tray holding meat and rice as well as potato or macaroni salad and costing from $6 to $10. *Bento* is the Japanese equivalent, with mixed meats and rice, while in Filipino diners you'll be offered *adobo*, pork or chicken stewed with garlic and vinegar. Korean barbecue, *kal bi* – prepared with sesame – is especially tasty, while *saimin* (pronounced *sy-min*), a bowl of clear soup filled with noodles and other ingredients, has become something of a national dish. Finally, the carbohydrate-packed *loco moco* is a fried egg served on a hamburger with gravy and rice.

Food in general is often referred to as *kaukau*, and it's also worth knowing that *pupus* (pronounced *poo-poos*) is a general term for little snacks, the kind of finger food that is given away in early-evening happy hours.

Lū'aus

These days, there's no such thing as an authentic "Hawaiian" restaurant; the closest you can come to eating traditional foods is at a **lū'au**. Primarily tourist money-spinners, and always accompanied by pseudo-Polynesian entertainment, these offer the chance to sample such dishes as *kālua* pork, an entire pig wrapped in *ti* leaves and baked all day in an underground oven;

Oahu *lū'aus*

Germaine's Ko Olina Resort, Kapolei ☎808/949-6626 or 1-800/367-5655, ✆www.germainesluau.com. Daily. $65. See p.161.
Paradise Cove Ko Olina Resort, Kapolei ☎808/842-5911 or 1-800/775-2683, ✆www.paradisecove.com. Daily. $73. See p.161.
Polynesian Cultural Center Lā'ie ☎808/293-3333 or 1-800/367-7060, ✆www.polynesia.com. Mon–Sat. $80. See p.140.
Royal Hawaiian Hotel Waikīkī ☎808/931-8383 or 921-4600. Mon. $99. See p.61.

poke, which is raw fish, shellfish, or octopus, marinated with soy and oriental seasonings; *poi*, a purple-gray paste produced by pounding the root of the *taro* plant; and *lomi-lomi*, a dish made with raw salmon. As *lū'aus* always involve mass catering and canteen-style self-service, the food itself is not sufficient incentive to go.

Fine dining

In the last few years, a distinctive new Hawaiian cuisine has emerged, known variously as **Pacific Rim**, **Euro-Asian**, or **Hawaii Regional**. In its ideal form it consists of combining foods and techniques from all the countries and ethnic groups that have figured in Hawaiian history, using the freshest ingredients possible. Top chefs, like Roy Yamaguchi of *Roy's*, preserve natural flavors by flash-frying meat and fish like the Chinese, baking it whole like the Hawaiians or even serving it raw like the Japanese. The effect is enhanced with Thai herbs and spices, and by the inventiveness of modern Californian cooking.

Surprisingly, Waikīkī has traditionally been somewhat short of top-class restaurants. The big-name chefs have tended to cook in Honolulu itself rather than Waikīkī, and some of the city's very best restaurants, such as *Alan Wong's*, are still located in residential areas where few tourists stray. More recently, however, more prestigious restaurants have started to open in the major Waikīkī hotels, including Sansei at the Marriott and Nobu at the Waikīkī Parc.

Drinks

The usual range of wines (mostly Californian) and beers is sold at Oahu restaurants and bars. At some point, however, every visitor seems to insist on getting wiped out by a tropical cocktail or two. Among the most popular are the Mai Tai, which should contain at least two kinds of rum, together with orange curacao and lemon juice; the Blue Hawaii, in which vodka is colored with blue curacao; and the Planter's Punch, made with light rum, grenadine, bitters and lemon juice.

Tap water is safe to drink. If you're hiking, however, never drink untreated stream water.

Tours

Bus tours

Countless operators in Waikīkī, such as Polynesian Adventure Tours (☎808/833-3000 or 1-800/622-3011, ⓦwww .polyad.com), E Noa Tours (☎808/591-2561 or 1-800/824-8804, ⓦwww.enoa .com), and Roberts (☎808/954-8652 or 1-866/898-2519, ⓦwww.robertshawaii .com), advertise **bus tours** of Honolulu and Oahu. Typical choices range from $22 for an excursion to Pearl Harbor, or $30 for a half-day tour of Pearl Harbor and downtown Honolulu, up to something around $60 for a full-day island tour, or up to $90 if you want to stop at destinations like Wainea Valley or the Polynesian Cultural Center.

Walking tours

Perhaps because Waikīkī and downtown Honolulu are so easy to explore on your own, few organized **walking tours** are available. As well as the tours of Chinatown detailed on p.81, however, it's also possible, on the first Friday of each month, to join free tours of either the central downtown area, or the Royal Mausoleum neighborhood near the Pali Highway (see p.109), which rendezvous at the Damien Statue outside the State Capitol at 1pm (☎808/948-3299).

For more energetic **hiking**, in different areas all over the island, the Hawaii chapter of the Sierra Club sponsors treks and similar activities on weekends (☎808/538-6616, ⓦwww .hi.sierraclub.org), while the Hawaii Nature Center arranges hikes most weekends (☎808/955-0100, ⓦwww .hawaiinaturecenter.org). Likehike (☎808/455-8193, www.gayhawaii.com /likehike) is a gay hiking club that runs group hikes on alternate Sundays. On the first Saturday and Sunday of each month, the Clean Air Team (☎808/948-3299) organizes two free hikes, one up **Diamond Head** and one to Diamond Head Lighthouse; both meet at 1pm in front of Honolulu Zoo.

Ocean sports and activities

With its palm-fringed sandy beaches and turquoise ocean, the opportunities for sea sports on Oahu are almost infinite, ranging from swimming through snorkeling, scuba diving, fishing, and whale-watching, to Hawaii's greatest gift to the world, the art of surfing.

If you're prepared to shop around a little, you can find much lower rates for most activities than those quoted by the operators; look for discount coupons in the free magazines, and in the handbills distributed on every street corner. You can also buy tickets for every conceivable island activity from the many independent "**activity centers**" in Waikīkī, such as *Aloha Express* (☎ 808/924-4030), *Hawaii Tour & Travels* (☎ 808/922-4884, ⓦ www .hawaiitourandtravels.com), *Magnum Tickets & Tours* (☎ 808/923-7825), and *Tours 4 Less* (☎ 808/923-2211). For activities not based in central Waikīkī, the price should include round-trip transport to the departure point.

Surfing

The nation that invented **surfing** – long before the foreigners came – remains its greatest arena. A recurring theme in ancient legends has young men frittering away endless days in the waves rather than facing up to their duties; now young people from all over the world flock to Hawaii to do just that. The sport was popularized early in the twentieth century by champion Olympic swimmer Duke Kahanamoku, the original Waikīkī Beach Boy; see p.49. He toured the world with his sixteen-foot board, demonstrating his skills to admiring crowds, and was responsible for introducing surfing to Australia.

Waikīkī lost its best surf breaks when it was relandscaped at the start of the tourist boom. Today, with advances in techniques and technology, surfing has never been more popular. Oahu's fabled North Shore is a Mecca for surf bums, who ride the waves around Sunset Beach and hang out in the coffee bars of Hale'iwa. However, surfing at such legendary sites is for experts only. Whatever your surfing experience at home, you need to be very sure you're up to it before you have a go in Hawaii, so start by sampling conditions at lesser surf-spots to be found on all the islands.

Concession stands near the Duke Kahanamoku statue in central Waikīkī rent out surfboards for around $10 per hour, and offer surfing lessons for beginners costing more like $40 per hour, including board rental. Lessons are great fun, and they really work; with the aid of a friendly push at the right moment, almost everyone manages to ride a wave within the hour.

Windsurfing

Since Oahu's Robby Naish won the first world championship in the 1970s, at the age of 13, Hawaii has also been recognized as the spiritual home of **windsurfing**. Maui tends to be regarded as the prime goal for enthusiasts from around the world, but Oahu also has some excellent spots, not least Kailua Beach on the windward shore (see p.131). Once again, be warned that Hawaiian waters present challenges on a vastly different scale from what you may be familiar with at home.

Among operators offering windsurfing lessons (from $75 for 2hr) and equipment rental (from $55 per half-day) at Kailua Beach are Hawaiian Watersports (☎ 808/262-5483, ⓦ www .hawaiianwatersports.com) and Kailua Sailboards and Kayaks (☎ 808/262-2555, www.kailuasailboards.com). A similar service on the North Shore is provided by Surf'n'Sea, 62-595 Kamehameha Hwy, Hale'iwa (☎808/637-9887 or 1-800/899-SURF, www.surfnsea.com); see p.149.

Snorkeling

Probably the easiest ocean activity for beginners is **snorkeling**. Equipped with mask, snorkel, and fins, you can while away hours and days having face-to-face encounters with the rainbow-colored populations of Hawaii's reefs and lava pools. A description of Oahu's best-known site,

Hanauma Bay, appears on p.122. As a rule, conditions in the waters close to Waikīkī tend to be less enticing; the best spot in the vicinity is Sans Souci Beach (see p.65).

Operators of snorkel cruises and similar activities provide equipment to their customers, and there's a concession stand at Hanauma Bay, but you may prefer to rent better stuff from a specialist such as Snorkel Bob's, 700 Kapahulu Ave, Waikīkī (☎808/735-7944, www.snorkelbob.com), or Surf'n'Sea in Hale'iwa (see p.149). Rates start as low as $9 per week.

Dinner and sightseeing cruises

Ali'i Kai Catamaran (☎808/954-8652 or 1-888/898-2519, www.robertshawaii .com). This giant catamaran offers kitsch sunset dinner cruises along Waikīkī Beach, leaving from Pier 5, near Honolulu's Aloha Tower, at 5.30pm daily. $61, ages 3–11 $33.

Navatek I (☎808/973-1311, www.atlantisadventures.com). Giant, very smooth-sailing catamaran, based at Pier 6 in Honolulu, which provides evening dinner cruises, complete with bland entertainment (poor-quality buffet $67.50, ages 2–12 $45; slightly better formal dining $94.50, ages 2–12 $60), and also a lunch buffet cruise, which include whale-watching in winter ($52, ages 2–12 $26)

Outrigger Catamaran (☎808/922-2210). Regular departures from Halekūlani Beach, immediately in front of Waikīkī 's *Outrigger Reef* hotel, including ninety-minute sunset and sail-powered trips for $35, and longer snorkel cruises for $45, plus whale-watching in winter.

Star of Honolulu (☎808/983-7827 or 1-800/334-6191, www.starofhonolulu .com). The cost of a dinner cruise on this enormous ship, which leaves from pier 8 beside Aloha Tower, depends on which of its four decks you opt for. The seven-course French dinner with jazz on the top deck is $169, with no child reductions; all other passengers get to see the same Polynesian revue, with a steak-and-lobster dinner on decks 2 and 3 costing $199 for adults, $71 for kids, and dinner on the bottom deck costing $69.50 (kids $41.50) or $47.50 ($28.50) depending on whether you want crab or chicken with your steak. Daytime cruises are cheaper, with 2hr whale-watching trips at $24.50 per person in winter.

Submarines

Atlantis Submarines (☎808/973-9811 or 1-800/548-6262, www .atlantisadventures.com). On these memorable one-of-a-kind trips, passengers are ferried to a spot from a quay at the *Hilton Hawaiian Village*, about a mile off Waikīkī, to rendezvous with two separate submarines. The 64-seater (adults $102, under-12s, who must be at least three feet tall, $51) is a bit more comfortable than the 48-seater ($81/$40.50), but the 45min cruise on either is substantially the same, descending a hundred feet beneath the waves to pass a sunken airplane and an artificial reef before circling a full-size shipwreck, with a certainty of seeing colorful fish and a likelihood of spotting sharks and turtles. Prices tend to drop each day from lunchtime onwards.

Ocean sports and activities | ESSENTIALS

Oahu's golf courses

Ala Wai Golf Course, Honolulu; $40;	☎808/296-2000
Bayview Golf Links, Kāneʻohe; $62;	☎808/247-0451
Coral Creek Golf Course, ʻEwa Beach; $125;	☎808/441-4653
ʻEwa Villages Golf Course, ʻEwa Beach; $47;	☎808/681-0220
Hawaii Country Club, Wahiawā; $49;	☎808/621-5654
Hawaii Kai Golf Course	
Championship Course, Hawaii Kai; $90;	☎808/395-2358
Executive Course, Hawaii Kai; $28.50;	☎808/395-2358
Hawaii Prince Golf Club, ʻEwa Beach; $135;	☎808/689-2213
Honolulu Country Club, Honolulu; $55;	☎808/833-4541
Kahuku Golf Course, North Shore; $20;	☎808/293-5842
Kapolei Golf Course, Ko ʻOlina; $70;	☎808/674-2227
Koʻolau Golf Course, Kāneʻohe; $145;	☎808/236-4653
Ko ʻOlina Golf Club, Ko ʻOlina; $165;	☎808/676-5300
Luana Hills Country Club, Kailua; $125;	☎808/262-2139
Mākaha Resort Golf Club, Mākaha; $160;	☎808/695-7519
Mākaha Valley Country Club, Mākaha; $80;	☎808/695-7111
Mililani Golf Club, Mililani; $99;	☎808/623-2222
Moanalua Golf Club, Honolulu; $20;	☎808/839-2311
New ʻEwa Beach Golf Club, ʻEwa Beach; $135;	☎808/689-8317
Olomana Golf Links, Waimānalo; $80;	☎808/259-7926
Pali Golf Course, Kāneʻohe; $42;	☎808/266-7612
Pearl Country Club, ʻAiea; $75;	☎808/487-3802
Ted Makalena Golf Course, Waipahu; $42;	☎808/675-6052
Turtle Bay Resort	
Fazio Course, Kahuku; $155;	☎808/293-8574
Palmer Course, Kahuku; $175;	☎808/293-8574
Waikele Golf Club, Waipahu; $100;	☎808/676-9000
West Loch Golf Course, ʻEwa Beach; $42;	☎808/296-2000

Diving

A typical rate for a two-tank scuba-diving boat trip on Oahu is $100. The best sites near Waikīkī are the wrecks visited by Atlantis Submarines, as described above; otherwise Waiʻanae in the west offers good conditions, Hanauma Bay makes a good shore dive, and there are various fine sites on the North Shore that can only be dived in summer. Operators include the Aloha Dive Shop at Koko Marina, not far from Hanauma Bay (☎808/395-5922, ⓦ www.alohadiveshop.com); SurfʼnʼSea in Haleʻiwa (☎808/637-3337 or 1-800/899-7873, ⓦ www.surfnsea .com); and Ocean Concepts in Waiʻanae (☎808/677-7975 or 1-800/808-3483, ⓦ www.oceanconcepts.com). An unusual variation is offered by Bob's Hawaii Adventure at Koko Marina (☎808/943-8628); no diving experience is required to take a half-hour ride along the ocean floor on an underwater moped, for $120.

Other watersports

Surfboard rental, surfing lessons, and outrigger canoe rides in Waikīkī are detailed on p.48; for details of Surf ʼnʼ

Sea, the North Shore's major operator, see p.149. The best place on Oahu to rent a kayak is Kailua Bay on the Windward Coast; for details of operators, see p.131. You can parasail off Waikīkī, although the boats set off from Kewalo Basin to the west, with Aloha Parasail (☎ 808/521-2446) or Hawaiian Parasail (☎ 808/591-1280), or in Koko Marina with Hawaii Watersports Center, with whom you can also waterski (☎ 808/395-3773, ⓦ www.hawaiiwatersportscenter.com).

Entertainment

Tourists staying in Waikīkī will find plenty of resort entertainment on offer, with (often free) Hawaiian music performances as well as theatrical spectaculars and live gigs in other genres. In addition, Waikīkī also has plenty of nightclubs, geared more towards younger tastes in music. Nightlife in the rest of Honolulu is more diverse, ranging from some very upscale clubs catering for wealthy urban professionals to a grungier scene for surfers and students who wouldn't be seen dead in Waikīkī .

If it's Hawaiian entertainment that interests you, that's not hard to find in Waikīkī, with most of the grander hotels featuring accomplished Hawaiian musicians most evenings. The *Halekūlani* is particularly recommended for its lovely setting, while some of the musicians themselves are very good indeed; Auntie Genoa Keawe at the *Waikīkī Beach Marriott* is absolutely unmissable (see p.61). It's also well worth looking out for events away from Waikīkī that are arranged for Hawaiian, rather than tourist, audiences, such as the frequent one-off performances and benefit concerts at downtown's beautiful Hawaii Theatre (see p.81), and Eddie Kamae's jam sessions at *Honey's* on the windward side of the island (see p.140).

The best regular free shows of Hawaiian music are given by the Royal Hawaiian Band (ⓦ www.royalhawaiianband.com), which, throughout the year except August, gives hour-long performances on Fridays at noon on the lawns of 'Iolani Palace downtown, and Sundays at 2pm in Waikīkī's Kapi'olani Park.

Various magazines and papers will keep you abreast of what's going on; the best are the free *Honolulu Weekly* newspaper (ⓦ www.honoluluweekly.com), and the *TGIF* section of Friday's *Honolulu Advertiser* (ⓦ www.honoluluadvertiser.com).

Festivals and events

Note that the exact dates of surfing contests, and in some cases the venues as well, depend on the state of the waves.

early Jan International Bodyboarding Association World Tour, Banzai Pipeline

mid-Jan Pacific Island Arts Festival, Thomas Square, facing Honolulu Academy of Arts

late Jan Pipeline Pro surfing competition, 'Ehukai Beach Park

Jan/Feb Narcissus Festival and Chinese New Year, Chinatown

early Feb NFL Pro Bowl, Aloha Stadium, Honolulu

Feb Buffalo's Big Board Surfing Classic, Mākaha Beach

third Mon in Feb Presidents' Day; Great Aloha Run, from Aloha Tower to Aloha Stadium.

early March Honolulu festival, downtown Honolulu

mid-March Hawaii Music Awards Week, Waikīkī

March 17 St Patrick's Day Parade, Waikīkī

March 26 Honolulu celebrations mark Prince Kūhio Day, state holiday

Easter Sunday Easter Sunrise Service at dawn, Punchbowl, Honolulu

May 1 Lei Day; public holiday, statewide celebrations

May 2 *Lei* ceremony at Royal Mausoleum, Honolulu

late May Molokai–Oahu kayak race ends at Hawaii Kai

late May Maui–Oahu Bankoh Ho'omana'o canoe race ends at Waikīkī Beach

June 11 Kamehameha Day; public holiday, statewide celebrations, Honolulu to Waikīkī parade

late June King Kamehameha *Hula* Festival, Blaisdell Center, Honolulu

late June Taste of Honolulu food festival, Civic Center Grounds, Honolulu

mid-July Hawaii International Jazz Festival, Honolulu

third Sat in July Prince Lot *Hula* Festival, Moanalua Gardens, Honolulu

early Aug State Farm Fair, Aloha Stadium, Honolulu

mid-Sept Aloha Festival, island-wide

late Sept Molokai–Oahu women's outrigger canoe race ends at Waikīkī

early Oct Molokai–Oahu men's outrigger canoe race ends at Waikīkī

Oct 31 Halloween parade, Waikīkī

first 2 wks Nov Hawaii International Film Festival, Honolulu

mid-Nov World Invitational *Hula* Festival, Honolulu

mid-Nov Triple Crown of Surfing; Hawaiian Pro, Ali'i Beach Park, Hale'iwa

late Nov/early Dec Triple Crown of Surfing; World Cup, Sunset Beach

early Dec Triple Crown of Surfing; Pipe Masters, Banzai Pipeline

second Sun in Dec Honolulu Marathon

Dec 25 Christmas Day; Aloha Bowl Football Classic, Aloha Stadium, Honolulu

Shopping

Many tourists come to Honolulu – where virtually all the shops are in convenient, purpose-built malls – exclusively for the **shopping**. For many years, the city's Ala Moana Center held undisputed sway as the premier mall for serious shoppers, but it has been so successful in attracting big spenders that rivals are springing up all the time. Even Waikīkī has started to expand beyond its traditional emphasis on souvenirs and beach accessories: wintertime window displays of distinctly un-Island-style fur coats and tweed bootcut trousers make an incongruous sight just blocks away from the ocean. That said, shoppers who are less interested in scooping up bargains from aseptic chains, and who are longing to buy a splashy T-shirt, a beach mat, or a monkey carved out of a coconut, will find plenty to satisfy them in **Waikīkī**. Kalākaua and Kūhio avenues especially are lined with cut-price souvenir stores; there are 37 shops in the ABC chain alone, all open daily from 6.30am to 1am and selling basic groceries as well as souvenir essentials.

Hawaiian crafts

Some of the most attractive products of Hawaii are just too ephemeral to take home. That goes for the orchids and tropical flowers on sale everywhere, and unfortunately it's also true of *leis*.

Leis (pronounced *lays*) are flamboyant decorative garlands, usually consisting of flowers such as the fragrant *melia* (the plumeria or frangipani) or the Big Island's own bright-red *lehua* blossom (from the *'ō'hia* tree), but sometimes also made from feathers, shells, seeds, or nuts. Both men and women wear them, above all on celebrations or gala occasions. The days are gone when every arriving tourist was festooned with a *lei*, but you'll probably be way-*leied* at a *lū'au* or some such occasion, while on Lei Day (May 1) everyone's at it.

Colorful **Hawaiian clothing**, such as *aloha* shirts and the cover-all "Mother-Hubbard"-style *mu'umu'u*

dress, is on sale everywhere, though classic designs are surprisingly rare and you tend to see the same stylized prints over and over again. The prevailing trend these days is for muted "reverse-print" designs, in which the cloth is effectively worn inside-out; for more stimulating ideas, seek out clothing designed by Sig Zane from the Big Island, who depicts spiritually significant Hawaiian plants and animals using traditional colors and dyes, or Tori Richard, whose fabrics have a playful, contemporary garishness.

Otherwise, the main **local crafts** are *lau hala* weaving, in which mats, hats, baskets, and the like are created by plaiting the large leaves (*lau*) of the spindly-legged pandanus (*hala*) tree, and wood turning, with fine bowls made from native dark woods such as *koa*.

Directory

Area code The telephone area code for the state of Hawaii is ☎808.

Electricity Hawaii's electricity supply, like that on the US mainland, uses 100 volts AC. Plugs are standard American two-pins.

Gay and lesbian life Much the greatest concentration of gay activism in Hawaii is in Honolulu, though the state as a whole is liberal on gay issues. It's one of 25 states to allow consensual "sodomy," with no criminal laws against private sex acts and a guarantee of privacy in the constitution. For general information on gay life in Honolulu, contact the Center, 614 South St, Honolulu (☎808/951-7000, ☻http://thecenterhawaii.org).

Honolulu's gay scene remains focused on **Kūhiō Avenue** in central Waikīkī, which houses most of Oahu's best-known gay businesses. For gay travelers, an evening at the legendary *Hula's Bar and Lei Stand* is the obvious first step. Step two would be to join the weekly **catamaran cruise** organized by Angles on Sundays at 1pm (☎808/926-9766, ☻www.angleswaikiki.com; $25).

Pacific Ocean Holidays (PO Box 88245, Honolulu HI 96830-8245; ☎808/944-4700 or 1-800/735-6600, ☻http://gayhawaiivacations.com) organizes all-inclusive **package vacations** in Hawaii for gay and lesbian travelers, and maintains the useful ☻www.gayhawaii.com website. Taking The Plunge (☎808/922-2600, ☻www.takemediving.com) is a highly recommended gay-friendly **scuba diving** company, while a gay **hiking** club, Likehike (☎808/455-8193, ☻www.gayhawaii.com /likehike), organizes different group hikes on alternate Sundays.

Hospitals Honolulu hospitals providing 24-hour assistance include Kuakini Medical Center, 347 Kuakini St (☎808/536-2236); Moanalua Medical Center, 3288 Moanalua Rd (☎808/834-5333); the Queens Medical Center, 1301 Punchbowl St (☎808/538-9011); and the Straub Clinic and Hospital, 888 S King St (☎808/522-4000). In emergencies call ☎911.

Inoculations No inoculations or vaccinations are required by law in order to enter Hawaii, though some authorities suggest a polio vaccination.

Fly Less – Stay Longer!

Rough Guides believes in the good that travel does, but we are deeply aware of the impact of fuel emissions on climate change. We recommend taking fewer trips and staying for longer. If you can avoid travelling by air, please use an alternative, especially for journeys of under 1000km/600miles. And always offset your travel at ⓦwww.roughguides.com/climatechange.

Mail Honolulu's main **post office**, facing the inter-island terminal at the airport at 3600 Aolele St, Honolulu, HI 96820 (Mon–Fri 7.30am–8.30pm, Sat 8am–4.30pm), is the only one in the city that accepts **general delivery** (poste restante) mail. There are other post offices at 330 Saratoga Rd in Waikīkī (Mon, Tues, Thurs & Fri 8am–4.30pm, Wed 8am–6pm, Sat 9am–noon); at the Ala Moana shopping mall (Mon–Fri 8.30am–5pm, Sat 8.30am–4.15pm); and downtown in the Old Federal Building at 335 Merchant St (Mon, Tues, Thurs & Fri 8am–4.30pm, Wed 8am–6pm).

Public restrooms Some public restrooms are labeled in Hawaiian: *Kanes* means Men, *Wahines* means Women.

Quarantine Very stringent restrictions apply to the importation of all plants and animals into Hawaii. Cats and dogs must stay in quarantine for 120 days; if you were hoping to bring an alligator or a hamster into the state, forget it. For full regulations call ☎808/871-5656.

Senior travelers US residents aged 50 or over can join the American Association of Retired Persons, 601 E St NW, Washington, DC 20049 (☎1-800/424-3410, ⓦwww .aarp.org), for discounts on accommodation and vehicle rental.

Time Unlike most of the United States, Hawaii does not observe Daylight Saving Time. Therefore, from 2am on the last Sunday in April until 2am on the last Sunday in October, the time difference between Hawaii and the US West Coast is three hours, not the usual two; the difference between Hawaii and the mountain region is four hours, not three;

and the islands are six hours later than the East Coast, not five. Hawaiian time is from ten to eleven hours behind the UK. In fact it's behind just about everywhere else; although New Zealand and Australia might seem to be two and four hours respectively behind Maui time, they're on the other side of the International Date Line, so are actually almost a full day ahead.

Tipping Waiting staff in restaurants expect tips of fifteen percent, in bars a little less. Hotel porters and bellhops should receive around $2 per piece of luggage and housekeeping staff $2 per night.

Travelers with disabilities The State of Hawaii Disability and Communication Access Board produces a wide range of reports on facilities for disabled travelers on each of the islands, which you can download from their website (☎808/586-8121, ⓦwww.state.hi.us/health/dcab/). In addition, Access–Able (ⓦwww .access–able.com) carries detailed reports on the accessibility of hotels and other facilities throughout Hawaii.

Weddings To get married in Hawaii, you must have a valid license, which costs $60 from the Department of Health, Marriage License Office, 1250 Punchbowl St, Honolulu HI 96813 (☎808/586-4545, ⓦwww .hawaii.gov/doh), and is valid for thirty days. To find an agent on Oahu who can issue a licence, call ☎808/586-4544. You also need proof of rubella immunizations or screening, which can be arranged through the Department of Health. Most resorts offer their own marriage planners, or you can pick up a full list of wedding services providers from the official state tourism website, ⓦwww.gohawaii.com.

Chronology

Chronology

c3.8 million years BC ▶ Volcanic eruptions cause Oahu to emerge from Pacific Ocean.

c10,000 BC ▶ Latest conceivable date for final eruption of Diamond Head volcano.

c200 AD ▶ First Polynesian voyagers reach Oahu from the Marquesas Islands; settlements at Kahana Valley and Bellows Field on the Windward coast.

c1000–c1300 ▶ Waves of Tahitian settlers arrive and violently displace their predecessors.

1778 ▶ British sailor Captain Cook glimpses Oahu before landing on Kauai and Niihau.

1779 ▶ Captain Cook again bypasses Oahu before meeting his death on the Big Island. His successor, Captain Clerke, subsequently puts in at Waimea Bay on Oahu's North Shore.

1792 ▶ Captain George Vancouver returns to find Oahu has been conquered by Chief Kahekili of Maui. Two of his crew are killed by warriors from the Pu'u O Mahuka Heiau.

1793 ▶ Captain William Brown, a British fur trader, finds a safe anchorage in southeastern Oahu. The Hawaiians know it as "He Awa Kou" or "the harbor of Kou," but Brown renames it "fair haven," which is soon translated into Hawaiian as "Honolulu."

1794 ▶ Kahekili himself dies at Waikīkī, and is succeeded by his son Kalanikūpule.

1795 ▶ Big Island chieftain Kamehameha invades Oahu and defeats Kalanikūpule's army in an epic battle at Nu'uanu.

1819 ▶ Kamehameha dies on the Big Island. By now Honolulu has become a thriving port.

1820 ▶ Puritan missionary Hiram Bingham arrives in Honolulu from New England.

1820s ▶ Whaling crews start to call in twice-yearly to pick up provisions, drop off their haul, and catch up on a little entertainment.

1843 ▶ A British commander captures Honolulu and claims Hawaii for Queen Victoria; six months later, word arrives from London that it has all been a mistake.

1845 ▶ After years of competition with Lahaina on Maui, Honolulu definitively becomes the capital of Hawaii.

1847 ▶ Sugar is now booming in the islands, with the industry largely controlled by the so-called Big Five: Hackfield & Co (later to become Amfac), C Brewer & Co, Theo Davies Co, Castle & Cooke (later Dole), and Alexander & Baldwin.

1848 ▶ In the Great Mahele, or "Division of Lands," King Kamehameha II permits private land ownership for the first time. Initially, all land is parceled out to native Hawaiians only, but much swiftly passes into the hands of the *haoles* (non-Hawaiians).

1857 ▶ Chinese laborers brought over to work in the sugar plantations of Kauai start to move to Oahu and set up their own businesses in Honolulu.

1872 ▶ The death of King Kamehameha V puts an end to the hereditary Kamehameha dynasty; from now on rulers are elected by the state legislature.

1874 ▶ King David Kalākaua, the "Merrie Monarch," ascends to the throne, amid riots at what's seen as his pro-American attitude. He reinstates public *hula* performances, discouraged by missionaries.

1876 ▶ A Treaty of Reciprocity abolishes all trade barriers and tariffs between the US and the Kingdom of Hawaii; sugar exports to the US increase tenfold within fifteen years.

1878 ▶ Portuguese settlers arive from Madeira and the Azores, bringing with them the little guitar-like *braguinha*, soon to become the ukulele.

1885 ▶ Joseph Kekuku, an 11-year-old Lāʻie schoolboy, slides a rod along the strings of his guitar and invents the steel guitar, later adopted by Delta blues musicians as well as Hawaiians.

1887 ▶ An armed, all-white group of "concerned businessmen" forces through the "Bayonet Constitution," in which the King surrenders power to an assembly elected by property owners (of any nationality) as opposed to citizens. The US government is swiftly granted exclusive rights to develop Pearl Harbor as a port.

1891 ▶ King Kalākaua dies in San Francisco, and is succeeded by his sister Queen Liliʻuokalani.

1893 ▶ After Queen Liliʻuokalani expresses her desire for a new constitution, the same "concerned businessmen" call in the US warship *Boston*, visiting Honolulu, and declare a provisional government.

1894 ▶ Although US President Grover Cleveland has demanded the restoration of the monarchy, the provisional government declares Hawaii a republic on July 4, with Sanford Dole as its first President.

1895 ▶ Queen Liliʻuokalani is charged with treason following an abortive coup attempt, and is placed under house arrest in ʻIolani Palace.

1898 ▶ Hawaii is formally annexed as a territory of the United States on August 12.

1898 ▶ The US also annexes the Phillipines; Filipinos soon arrive in Honolulu in great numbers.

1900 ▶ Controlled fires intended to suppress an outbreak of plague burn down most of Chinatown.

1901 ▶ The four-story, 74-room *Moana Hotel* opens in Waikīkī.

1902 ▶ Korean immigrants reach Honolulu.

1907 ▶ Under the Gentleman's Agreement, further immigration from Japan is banned.

1912 ▶ Waikīkī "Beachboy" Duke Kahanamoku wins Olympic swimming gold, and tours the world popularizing surfing.

1926 ▸ The newly completed Aloha Tower stands as Honolulu's tallest building.

1927 ▸ The *Royal Hawaiian*, or "Pink Palace," opens in Waikīkī.

1935 ▸ The "Hawaii Calls" radio program commences worldwide broadcasts from the *Moana Hotel*.

1936 ▸ The first commercial flight from San Francisco reaches Honolulu.

1941 ▸ A surprise Japanese aerial attack on Pearl Harbor on December 7 kills 2403 military personnel, and precipitates US entry into World War II.

1946 ▸ Following decades of union activity, Hawaii's plantation workers win their first victory, and will soon become the highest paid agricultural laborers in the world. The long-term Republican domination of state politics is about to end.

1959 ▸ Hawaii finally becomes the fiftieth of the United States. The only significant opposition comes from the few remaining native Hawaiians. Statehood coincides with the first jet flight to Hawaii, triggering a boom in tourism.

1960 ▸ Led by slack-key guitarist Gabby Pahinui and ukulele maestro Eddie Kamae, the Sons of Hawaii play their first gig in Honolulu, spearheading a revival of interest in Hawaiian music.

1961 ▸ Elvis Presley releases the movie *Blue Hawaii*, and makes his first post-army concert appearance a benefit show for the *USS Arizona* memorial in Pearl Harbor.

1973 ▸ Elvis Presley's *Aloha from Hawaii* concert special, filmed in what's now the Blaisdell Center, is broadcast by satellite to a global audience of over a billion people.

1976 ▸ On its maiden voyage, the *Hōkūleʻa* canoe sails to Tahiti in thirty days, sparking a new interest and pride in the achievements of ancient Polynesian navigators, and inspiring political activists calling for Hawaiian Sovereignty.

1991 ▸ Honolulu's Dole pineapple cannery, once the largest in the world, closes down.

1993 ▸ President Clinton acknowledges the illegality of the US overthrow of the Hawaiian monarchy with an official apology to Native Hawaiians.

1997 ▸ Much-loved singer Israel Kamakawiwoʻole dies aged 38, and is given a state funeral.

2006 ▸ Del Monte announces that it will harvest its last crop of pineapples on Oahu in 2008, leaving Dole as the island's only pineapple producer.

Travel store

Available from all good bookstores D: Rough Guide DIRECTIONS

For more information go to www.roughguides.com

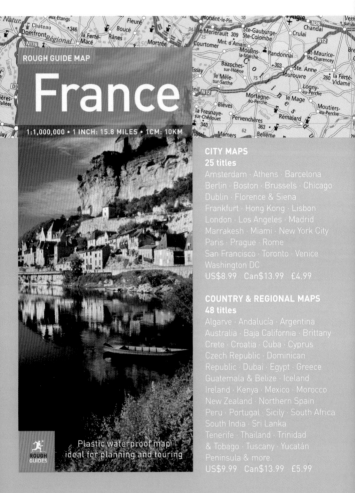

small print & Index

A Rough Guide to Rough Guides

In 1981, Mark Ellingham, a recent graduate in English from Bristol University, was travelling in Greece on a tiny budget and couldn't find the right guidebook. With a group of friends he wrote his own guide, combining a contemporary, journalistic style with a practical approach to travellers' needs. That first Rough Guide was a student scheme that became a publishing phenomenon. Today, Rough Guides include recommendations from shoestring to luxury and cover hundreds of destinations around the globe, including almost every country in the Americas and Europe, more than half of Africa and most of Asia and Australasia. Millions of readers relish Rough Guides' wit and inquisitiveness as much as their enthusiastic, critical approach and value-for-money ethos. The guides' ever-growing team of authors and photographers is spread all over the world.

In the early 1990s, Rough Guides branched out of travel, with the publication of Rough Guides to World Music, Classical Music and the Internet. All three have become benchmark titles in their fields, spearheading the publication of a range of more than 350 titles under the Rough Guide name, including phrasebooks, waterproof maps, music guides from Opera to Heavy Metal, reference works as diverse as Conspiracy Theories and Shakespeare, and popular culture books from iPods to Poker. Rough Guides also produce a series of more than 120 World Music CDs in partnership with World Music Network.

Visit www.roughguides.com to see our latest publications.

Rough Guide travel images are available for commercial licensing at www.roughguidespictures.com

Publishing information

This first edition published **October** 2007 by Rough Guides Ltd, 80 Strand, London WC2R 0RL. 345 Hudson St, 4th Floor, New York, NY 10014, USA.

Distributed by the Penguin Group
Penguin Books Ltd, 80 Strand, London WC2R 0RL
Penguin Group (USA), 375 Hudson Street, New York, NY 10014, USA
14 Local Shopping Centre, Panchsheel Park, New Delhi 110017, India
Penguin Group (Australia), 250 Camberwell Road, Camberwell, Victoria 3124, Australia
Penguin Group (Canada), 10 Alcorn Avenue, Toronto, ON M4V 1E4, Canada
Penguin Group (NZ), 67 Apollo Drive, Mairangi Bay, Auckland 1310, New Zealand
Typeset in Bembo and Helvetica to an original design by Henry Iles.
Cover concept by Peter Dyer.

Printed and bound in China

© Samantha Cook and Greg Ward 2007

No part of this book may be reproduced in any form without permission from the publisher except for the quotation of brief passages in reviews.

208pp includes index

A catalogue record for this book is available from the British Library

ISBN 978-1-84353-848-6

1   3   5   7   9   8   6   4   2

Help us update

We've gone to a lot of effort to ensure that the first edition of Honolulu DIRECTIONS is accurate and up-to-date. However, things change – places get "discovered", opening hours are notoriously fickle, restaurants and rooms raise prices or lower standards. If you feel we've got it wrong or left something out, we'd like to know, and if you can remember the address, the price, the phone number, so much the better.

We'll credit all contributions, and send a copy of the next edition (or any other DIRECTIONS guide or Rough Guide if you prefer) for the best letters. Everyone who writes to us and isn't already a subscriber will receive a copy of our full-colour thrice-yearly newsletter. Please mark letters: "Honolulu DIRECTIONS Update" and send to: Rough Guides, 80 Strand, London WC2R 0RL, or Rough Guides, 4th Floor, 345 Hudson St, New York, NY 10014. Or send an email to mail@ roughguides.com

Have your questions answered and tell others about your trip at www.roughguides.atinfopop.com

Rough Guide credits

Text editor: April Isaacs
Layout: Anita Singh
Photography: Greg Ward
Cartography: Katie Lloyd-Jones

Picture editor: Nicole Newman
Proofreader: Susannah Wight
Production: Aimee Hampson
Cover design: Chloë Roberts

SMALL PRINT

The authors

Greg Ward has covered Hawaii for Rough Guides since 1992, and is the sole author of the Rough Guide to Hawaii and of Maui Directions. He has also written and photographed several other Rough Guides, including those to the USA, the Southwest USA, Las Vegas, the Grand Canyon, Blues CDs, and US History, as well as covering Hawaii for other publishers. Samantha Cook has written Rough Guides to New Orleans, the USA, Online Travel and Chick Flicks, among others. She lives and works in London.

Acknowledgements

Greg and Sam would like to thank the many people who made researching this book such a pleasure, including Gina Baurile, Nancy Daniels, Barry Flanagan, Emele Freiberg, Kathy Hansberry, Stephanie Jucutan, Eddie Kamae, Denise Park, and Maria Quidez. Thanks also to the great team at Rough Guides, and especially our ever-patient editor April Isaacs, Steven Horak, Katie Lloyd-Jones, Nicole Newman, and Anita Singh.

Photo credits

Index

Maps are marked in color

j

k

l

m

i

INDEX